HOW TO READ BODY LANGUAGE

LANGUAGE

Unlock The Secrets of Effective Communication and Deepen Your Connections by Analyzing Nonverbal Signals.

Justin J. Williams

Table of Contents

Introduction

Welcome to HOW TO READ BODY LANGUAGE: Unlock the Secrets of Effective Communication and Deepen Your Connections by Analyzing Nonverbal Signals.

Have you ever found yourself in a situation where words seemed insufficient? I vividly recall an encounter that changed my perspective on communication. In a crowded room, the unspoken language between two people spoke volumes, and I realized the power that lies beyond spoken words.

This book is not just a guide; it's a journey born from that pivotal moment. Imagine being able to decipher the subtle cues that elude verbal expression, to connect with others on a level so profound that conversations become a dance of shared understanding.

In these pages, you'll discover the secrets to effective communication, grounded in the art of reading body language. We've all experienced the frustration of miscommunication, the disconnect that arises when words fail to convey the full spectrum of emotions. I've been there too, and it's this shared experience that fuels the passion behind this book.

Let's embark on a transformative exploration together, where each turn of the page brings you closer to unlocking the mysteries of nonverbal signals. HOW TO READ BODY LANGUAGE is not just about communication; it's about connection, empathy, and the shared human experience. Join me as we delve into a world where understanding goes beyond words, and connections deepen through the silent language we all share.

Chapter 1: Introduction to Body Language

What is Body Language?

Body language is a form of nonverbal communication that involves the use of physical movements, gestures, and facial expressions to convey information and express emotions. It is a powerful tool that can provide valuable insights into a person's thoughts, feelings, and intentions. Understanding body language can help you decode hidden messages, improve your communication skills, and build stronger connections with others.

The Importance of Body Language

Body language plays a crucial role in our everyday interactions. It is estimated that more than 70% of communication is nonverbal, meaning that the way we move, stand, and use our facial expressions can often speak louder than words. By paying attention to body language cues, we can gain a deeper understanding of what someone is saying, even when their words may be saying something different.

The Elements of Body Language

Body language is composed of various elements that work together to convey meaning. These elements include facial expressions, gestures, posture, eye contact, and touch. Each of these components can provide valuable information about a person's emotions, attitudes, and intentions.

Facial Expressions

Facial expressions are one of the most powerful and easily recognizable forms of body language. The human face is capable of expressing a wide range of emotions, including happiness, sadness, anger, fear, surprise, and disgust. By observing someone's facial expressions, you can gain insight into their emotional state and how they are reacting to a particular situation.

Gestures and Posture

Gestures and posture refer to the way we use our hands, arms, and body to communicate. They can include movements such as pointing, waving, crossing arms, or leaning forward. Posture, on the other hand, refers to the way we hold our body, whether it's standing tall and confident or slouching and closed off. These nonverbal cues can reveal a person's level of comfort, confidence, and engagement in a conversation.

Eye Contact and Gaze

Eye contact is a powerful form of nonverbal communication conveying trust, interest, and attentiveness. Making eye contact indicates that you are paying attention and participating in the conversation. However, the duration and intensity of eye contact can vary across cultures and contexts, so it's important to consider cultural norms when interpreting this nonverbal cue.

Touch and Personal Space

Touch is an effective nonverbal communication tool that can express a variety of feelings and intentions. A gentle touch on the arm can signal comfort and support, while a firm handshake can convey confidence and assertiveness. Personal space, on the other hand, refers to the physical distance we maintain between ourselves and others. Different cultures have different norms regarding personal space, so it's important to be mindful of these cultural differences when interpreting touch and personal space cues.

The Role of Body Language in Communication

Body language plays a crucial role in communication, as it can enhance or contradict the verbal messages we convey. For example, if someone says they are happy but their body language suggests otherwise, it can create confusion and mistrust. On the other hand, aligning our body language with our words can help to reinforce our message and build rapport with others.

Understanding body language can also help us to interpret the emotions and intentions of others more accurately. By paying attention to nonverbal cues, we can pick up on subtle signals that may indicate discomfort, deception, or interest. This can be particularly useful in situations where verbal communication may be limited, such as when interacting with someone who speaks a different language or when observing someone from a distance.

Body language is a powerful form of nonverbal communication that can provide valuable insights into a person's thoughts, feelings, and intentions. By understanding and interpreting body language cues, we can enhance our communication skills, build stronger connections with others, and navigate social interactions more effectively.

Why is Body Language Important?

In our everyday encounters, body language is an essential nonverbal communication tool. It is the unspoken language that conveys our thoughts, feelings, and intentions through facial expressions, gestures, postures, and other physical cues. Understanding and interpreting body language can provide valuable insights into a person's emotions, attitudes,

13

and intentions, allowing us to navigate social situations more effectively and build stronger connections with others.

Enhancing Communication

One of the primary reasons why body language is important is its ability to enhance communication. While verbal communication is essential, it is often the nonverbal cues that provide the true meaning behind the words spoken. For example, a person may say they are fine, but their crossed arms and tense facial expression may indicate otherwise. By paying attention to these nonverbal signals, we can gain a deeper understanding of what someone is truly feeling or thinking.

Body language also helps to fill in the communication gaps. In situations where language barriers exist or when words fail to fully express our thoughts and emotions, nonverbal cues become even more critical. A smile, a nod, or a pat on the back can convey warmth, agreement, or support without the need for words. By being attuned to these nonverbal signals, we can bridge the communication gap and foster better understanding.

Building Rapport and Trust

Body language plays a vital role in building rapport and establishing trust with others. When we can accurately interpret and respond to the nonverbal cues of those around us, we create a sense of connection and empathy. This can help to strengthen relationships, whether they are personal or professional.

For example, maintaining eye contact during a conversation signals attentiveness and interest, making the other person feel valued and heard. Similarly, open and relaxed body postures convey approachability and friendliness, making it easier for others to feel comfortable and open up. By using positive body language, we can create an environment of trust and openness, fostering stronger and more meaningful connections with others.

Understanding Emotions and Intentions

Body language provides valuable insights into a person's emotions and intentions. It allows us to gauge how someone is feeling, even when they may not explicitly express it verbally. For instance, crossed arms, furrowed brows, or a downturned mouth can indicate feelings of anger, frustration, or sadness. On the other hand, a relaxed posture, open palms, and a genuine smile can convey happiness, contentment, or friendliness.

By understanding these nonverbal cues, we can respond appropriately and effectively to the emotions of others. This can help us provide support, offer comfort, or adjust our behavior to create a more positive and harmonious interaction. Being able to accurately interpret body language can also help us assess someone's intentions, allowing us to make informed decisions and navigate social situations with greater confidence.

Detecting Deception

Another important aspect of body language is its role in detecting deception. While it is not a foolproof method, certain nonverbal cues can indicate when someone is being dishonest or hiding something. Microexpressions, for example, are fleeting facial expressions that can reveal true emotions, even when someone is trying to conceal them. Incongruence between verbal and nonverbal cues, such as avoiding eye contact or fidgeting, can also be indicators of deception.

By being aware of these deceptive body language signals, we can become more discerning and cautious in our interactions. This can be particularly useful in situations where trust is crucial, such as in negotiations, interviews, or personal relationships. However, it is important to note that body language should be considered in conjunction with other factors, as individual differences and cultural norms can influence nonverbal behavior.

Cultural Sensitivity and Adaptability

Lastly, body language is important because it helps us navigate cultural differences and promotes cultural sensitivity. Different cultures have their own unique set of nonverbal cues and gestures, and understanding these cultural nuances is essential for effective communication and avoiding misunderstandings.

For example, while direct eye contact is considered a sign of attentiveness and respect in Western cultures, it may be seen as disrespectful or confrontational in other cultures. Similarly, hand gestures that are innocuous in one culture may carry offensive meanings in another. By being aware of these cultural differences and adapting our body language accordingly, we can show respect and build positive relationships across cultures.

Body language is important because it enhances communication, builds rapport and trust, helps us understand emotions and intentions, aids in detecting deception, and promotes cultural sensitivity. By mastering the art of body language, we can become more effective communicators, build stronger connections with others, and navigate social situations with greater ease and confidence.

The Basics of Body Language

Body language is a powerful form of nonverbal communication that can reveal a person's thoughts, feelings, and intentions. It involves the use of facial expressions, gestures, posture, eye contact, and other physical cues to convey messages without the need for words. Understanding and interpreting body language can provide valuable insights into a person's true emotions and help improve communication and relationships.

Facial Expressions

Facial expressions are one of the most important aspects of body language. The face is incredibly expressive and can convey a wide range of emotions, including happiness, sadness, anger, fear, surprise, and disgust. By paying attention to someone's facial expressions, you can gain a deeper understanding of their emotional state.

A true grin, for instance, is characterized by the Duchenne smile, which is the contraction of the muscles surrounding the eyes. This type of smile indicates genuine happiness or joy. On the other hand, a forced smile, where only the muscles around the mouth are engaged, may indicate that someone is trying to hide their true emotions.

Gestures and Posture

Gestures and posture also play a significant role in body language. The way a person moves their body and positions themselves can provide valuable insights into their confidence, interest, and level of engagement.

For instance, open and relaxed body postures, such as uncrossed arms and legs, indicate that a person is open to communication and receptive to others. On the other hand, closed postures, such as crossed arms and legs, suggest defensiveness or discomfort.

Gestures can also convey specific meanings. For example, nodding the head while someone is speaking indicates agreement or understanding, while shaking the head from side to side indicates disagreement or disbelief. It's important to note that gestures can vary across cultures, so it's essential to consider cultural differences when interpreting them.

Eye Contact and Gaze

Eye contact is a powerful form of nonverbal communication that can convey interest, trust, and sincerity. Maintaining appropriate eye contact during a conversation shows that you are actively engaged and interested in what the other person is saying.

The meaning of eye contact can vary depending on the context and cultural norms. In some cultures, prolonged eye contact may be seen as a sign of respect and attentiveness, while in others, it may be considered rude or confrontational. It's important to be aware of these cultural differences when interpreting eye contact.

Gaze direction is another important aspect of body language. The direction in which a person looks can indicate their level of interest or attraction. For example, if someone is looking directly at you during a conversation, it suggests that they are fully engaged and interested in what you have to say. On the other hand, if their gaze is constantly shifting or avoiding eye contact, it may indicate discomfort or disinterest.

Proxemics and Personal Space

The study of proxemics is the use and perception of personal space by individuals. The distance we maintain between ourselves and others can convey important messages about our relationships and level of comfort.

Different cultures have different norms regarding personal space. In some cultures, people stand closer together during conversations, while in others, a larger personal space is preferred. Violating someone's personal space can make them feel uncomfortable or threatened, so it's important to be mindful of these cultural differences.

Understanding the basics of body language is essential for effective communication and building strong relationships. By paying attention to facial expressions, gestures, posture, eye contact, and personal space, you can gain valuable insights into a person's thoughts, feelings, and intentions.

It's important to remember that body language is not an exact science and should be interpreted in conjunction with other verbal and nonverbal cues. With practice and observation, you can become more skilled at reading and interpreting body language, enhancing your communication skills and improving your interactions with others.

Common Body Language Signals

Body language is a powerful form of nonverbal communication that can reveal a person's thoughts, feelings, and intentions. By understanding and interpreting common body language signals, you can gain valuable insights into the emotions and attitudes of others. In this section, we will explore some of the most common body language signals and what they typically indicate.

Facial Expressions

Facial expressions are one of the most noticeable and easily interpreted forms of body language. The face is incredibly expressive and can convey a wide range of emotions. The following list of popular face expressions and their meanings:

Smiling: A genuine smile indicates happiness, friendliness, and warmth. It involves the corners of the mouth turning up and the eyes crinkling.

Frowning: A furrowed brow and downturned mouth indicate sadness, anger, or frustration.

Raised eyebrows: Raised eyebrows can indicate surprise, disbelief, or interest.

Narrowed eyes: Narrowed eyes can indicate suspicion, skepticism, or anger.

Eye rolling: Rolling one's eyes is a sign of annoyance, frustration, or disbelief.

Pursed lips: Pursed lips can indicate disapproval, disagreement, or tension.

Gestures and Posture

Gestures and posture can provide valuable information about a person's confidence, comfort level, and engagement in a conversation. Here are some common gestures and postures and their meanings:

Open arms: Open arms, with palms facing forward, indicate openness, friendliness, and approachability.

Crossed arms: Crossed arms can indicate defensiveness, resistance, or discomfort.

Leaning forward: Leaning forward indicates interest, engagement, and attentiveness.

Leaning back: Leaning back can indicate relaxation, disinterest, or a desire to create distance.

Nodding: Nodding indicates agreement, understanding, and active listening.

Shrugging: Shrugging the shoulders can indicate uncertainty, confusion, or a lack of knowledge.

Eye Contact and Gaze

Eye contact is a crucial aspect of nonverbal communication and can convey various messages depending on the context. Here are some common eye contact and gaze signals and their meanings:

Direct eye contact: Direct eye contact indicates confidence, honesty, and attentiveness.

Avoiding eye contact: Avoiding eye contact can indicate shyness, discomfort, or dishonesty.

Prolonged eye contact: Prolonged eye contact can indicate interest, attraction, or intimidation.

Glancing or darting eyes: Glancing or darting eyes can indicate nervousness, anxiety, or a lack of focus.

Touch and Personal Space

Touch and personal space are important aspects of body language that can vary greatly depending on cultural norms and individual preferences. Here are some common touch and personal space signals and their meanings:

Handshakes: A firm handshake indicates confidence and professionalism, while a weak handshake can indicate insecurity or disinterest.

Hugging: Hugging can indicate warmth, affection, and closeness.

Personal space: The distance someone maintains between themselves and others can indicate their comfort level. Standing too close can indicate aggression or invasion of personal space while standing too far away can indicate disinterest or discomfort.

Other Body Language Signals

In addition to the signals mentioned above, there are several other common body language signals that can provide insights into a person's thoughts and emotions. These include:

Leg and foot movements: Tapping feet, crossed legs, or restless leg movements can indicate impatience, nervousness, or discomfort.

Hand gestures: Hand gestures can emphasize points, convey enthusiasm, or indicate frustration.

Mirroring: Mirroring another person's body language can indicate rapport, agreement, and a desire to connect.

Posture: Slumped shoulders and a hunched back can indicate low confidence or a lack of energy, while an upright posture can indicate confidence and assertiveness.

By becoming familiar with these common body language signals, you can enhance your ability to understand and interpret the nonverbal cues of others. It is important to remember that body language is not an exact science and can vary from person to person. It is essential to consider the context, cultural differences, and individual differences when interpreting body language signals.

Chapter 2: Nonverbal Communication

Facial Expressions

One of the most crucial elements of nonverbal communication is facial expression. They play a crucial role in conveying emotions, thoughts, and intentions. Understanding facial expressions can give you valuable insights into a person's state of mind and help you decode their true feelings.

The Importance of Facial Expressions

Facial expressions are universal and can be understood across different cultures and languages. They are innate and instinctive, making them a reliable indicator of a person's emotional state. By paying attention to someone's facial expressions, you can gain a deeper understanding of their thoughts and feelings, even when they are not explicitly expressed through words.

The Basic Facial Expressions

Six basic facial expressions are universally recognized: happiness, sadness, anger, fear, surprise, and disgust. These expressions are hardwired into our brains and are easily recognizable, regardless of cultural background. Each expression is characterized by specific muscle movements and changes in the face.

Happiness: A genuine smile involves the contraction of the muscles around the eyes, known as the Duchenne smile. It is a sign of genuine happiness and is often accompanied by raised cheeks and an upward curve of the lips.

Sadness: The facial expression of sadness is characterized by a downward curve of the lips, drooping eyebrows, and a relaxed or tense appearance. Tears or runny eyes may be seen.

Anger: Anger is typically expressed through narrowed eyes, a furrowed brow, and a tense or clenched jaw. The lips may be pressed tightly together, and the face may appear flushed or red.

Fear: The facial expression of fear involves widened eyes, raised eyebrows, and a tense or startled appearance. The mouth may be slightly open, and the lips may be pulled back.

Surprise: Surprise is characterized by widened eyes, raised eyebrows, and an open mouth. The jaw may drop slightly, and the person may freeze momentarily.

Disgust: The expression of disgust involves a wrinkled nose, raised upper lip, and a slight narrowing of the eyes. The person may also turn their head away or cover their nose.

Microexpressions

Microexpressions are brief, involuntary facial expressions that occur in a fraction of a second. They are often a result of suppressed or concealed emotions. These microexpressions can provide valuable clues about a person's true feelings, as they are difficult to control or fake.

Microexpressions can be subtle and fleeting, making them challenging to detect. However, with practice and observation, you can train yourself to recognize these microexpressions and gain deeper insights into a person's emotions.

Cultural Differences in Facial Expressions

While facial expressions are generally universal, there can be some cultural variations in their interpretation. Different cultures may have specific facial expressions that are unique to their social norms and customs. For example, a smile may have different meanings in different cultures, ranging from politeness to genuine happiness.

It is essential to consider cultural context when interpreting facial expressions, especially in cross-cultural interactions. Being aware of these cultural differences can help avoid misinterpretation and misunderstandings.

Improving Your Facial Expression Reading Skills

Reading facial expressions accurately requires practice and observation. Here are some tips to improve your facial expression reading skills:

Observe: Pay close attention to people's facial expressions in different situations. Observe the subtle changes in their facial muscles and how they correspond to their emotions.

Practice: Look at yourself in the mirror and practice making different facial expressions. Pay attention to how each expression feels and the muscle movements involved.

Study: Read books or articles on facial expressions and nonverbal communication. Familiarize yourself with the different facial muscles and their corresponding expressions.

Context: Consider the context in which the facial expression occurs. The same expression can have different meanings depending on the situation and the person's cultural background.

Body Language: Pay attention to other nonverbal cues, such as body posture and gestures, to get a more comprehensive understanding of a person's emotions.

Empathy: Try to grasp the other person's point of view by placing yourself in their position. This will improve your ability to read their facial emotions.

By honing your skills in reading facial expressions, you can become more adept at understanding people's emotions and intentions. This can greatly enhance your communication skills and improve your relationships with others. Facial expressions are a powerful tool for decoding the hidden language of emotions.

Gestures and Postures

Gestures and posture are essential components of nonverbal communication. They play a significant role in conveying messages and emotions without the need for words. Understanding and interpreting gestures and posture can provide valuable insights into a person's thoughts, feelings, and intentions.

Hand Gestures

Hand gestures are one of the most common forms of nonverbal communication. They can vary greatly across cultures and individuals, but some gestures have universal meanings. For example, a thumbs-up gesture is generally understood as a sign of approval or agreement, while a raised middle finger is considered offensive in many cultures.

Hand gestures can also convey specific meanings depending on the context. For instance, a person may use a hand gesture to emphasize a point during a conversation or to signal that they want to speak. Paying attention to these gestures can help you better understand the speaker's intentions and emotions.

Posture

Posture refers to the way a person holds their body while standing, sitting, or moving. It can reveal a lot about a person's confidence, mood, and level of engagement. For example, someone with a slouched posture may appear disinterested or lacking in confidence, while someone with an upright and open posture may come across as confident and approachable.

Posture can also indicate power dynamics in social interactions. People in positions of authority often adopt a more expansive posture, taking up more space and displaying dominance. On the other hand, individuals who feel subordinate or intimidated may adopt a more closed and defensive posture, trying to make themselves appear smaller.

Facial Expressions and Body Language

Facial expressions and body language are closely intertwined with gestures and posture. They work together to convey emotions and intentions. For example, a smile can indicate happiness or friendliness, while a furrowed brow may signal confusion or concern.

When interpreting facial expressions and body language, it is crucial to consider the context and the individual's overall demeanor. A single gesture or expression may not provide a complete picture of someone's emotions or intentions. It is essential to observe multiple cues and look for consistency in their nonverbal signals.

Mirroring and Synchronization

Mirroring and synchronization are nonverbal behaviors that involve mimicking the gestures and postures of others. When people feel a connection or rapport with someone, they often unconsciously mirror their body language. This mirroring can create a sense of trust and rapport between individuals.

Synchronization goes beyond mirroring and involves matching the timing and rhythm of movements. For example, two people engaged in a conversation may synchronize their gestures and speech patterns. This synchronization can enhance communication and create a sense of harmony between individuals.

Cultural Differences in Gestures and Postures

It is important to note that gestures and posture can vary significantly across different cultures. What may be considered acceptable or even positive in one culture may be seen as offensive or disrespectful in another. For example, the "OK" hand gesture, which is commonly used to indicate approval or agreement in many Western cultures, can be offensive in some Middle Eastern countries.

To avoid misunderstandings and cultural faux pas, it is crucial to familiarize yourself with the cultural norms and practices of the people you interact with. Being aware of these differences can help you navigate cross-cultural communication more effectively and avoid unintentionally offending.

Interpreting Gestures and Postures in Context

When interpreting gestures and posture, it is essential to consider the context in which they occur. Different situations can influence the meaning and significance of nonverbal cues. For example, a person crossing their arms may indicate defensiveness or disagreement in a heated argument, but it could also simply mean they are feeling cold.

It is also important to remember that individual differences can influence nonverbal communication. Not everyone will display the same gestures or postures in the same situations. Personal preferences, cultural background, and personality traits can all influence how someone expresses themselves nonverbally.

Practicing Observation and Awareness

To become proficient in reading gestures and posture, it is essential to practice observation and awareness. Pay attention to the nonverbal cues of those around you, both in everyday interactions and in more formal settings. Observe how people's gestures and postures change in different situations and contexts.

Developing awareness of your nonverbal signals is also crucial. Pay attention to your gestures and posture and how they may be perceived by others. Practice adopting open and confident postures to enhance your communication and build rapport with others.

By honing your skills in reading and interpreting gestures and posture, you can gain valuable insights into the thoughts, feelings, and intentions of those around you. This understanding can enhance your communication skills, improve your relationships, and help you navigate social and professional interactions more effectively.

Eye Contact and Gaze

Eye contact is a powerful form of nonverbal communication that plays a significant role in our daily interactions. It is often said that the eyes are the windows to the soul, and this holds when it comes to understanding body language. The way someone looks at you or avoids looking at you, can convey a wealth of information about their thoughts, feelings, and intentions.

The Importance of Eye Contact

One essential component of human communication is eye contact. It establishes a connection between individuals and can convey a range of emotions and intentions. When someone maintains eye contact with you, it signals that they are interested, engaged, and paying attention to what you are saying. It creates a sense of trust and openness, fostering a deeper connection between people.

On the other hand, avoiding eye contact can indicate discomfort, shyness, or even deception. When someone avoids looking directly into your eyes, it may suggest that they are hiding something or feeling insecure. Lack of eye contact can also be a sign of disinterest or disrespect, as it can make the other person feel ignored or unimportant.

Different Types of Eye Contact

Not all eye contact is the same, and different types of eye contact can convey different messages. Here are a few common types of eye contact and their meanings:

Gaze: A gaze is a prolonged and intense form of eye contact. It is often associated with romantic or intimate connections. When someone gazes into your eyes, it can indicate attraction, desire, or a deep emotional bond.

Glances: Glances are quick and fleeting eye contact. They can be a sign of curiosity, interest, or even flirtation. Glances are often used to assess someone's appearance or to gauge their reaction to a particular situation.

Avoidance: Avoiding eye contact can have various meanings depending on the context. In some cultures, avoiding eye contact is a sign of respect or submission. In most situations, it suggests discomfort, lack of confidence, or dishonesty.

Staring: Staring is an intense and prolonged form of eye contact that can make people feel uncomfortable or threatened. It can be seen as intrusive or aggressive and is generally considered impolite. Staring can also indicate dominance or a desire to intimidate.

Cultural Differences in Eye Contact

It is important to note that the meaning and significance of eye contact can vary across different cultures. In some cultures, direct eye contact is considered respectful and a sign of attentiveness. It could be interpreted as aggressive or impolite by others. Therefore, it is crucial to be aware of cultural norms and adapt your behavior accordingly when interacting with individuals from different backgrounds.

For example, in Western cultures, maintaining eye contact during a conversation is generally seen as a sign of honesty and engagement. However, in many Asian cultures, prolonged eye contact can be seen as impolite or aggressive.

It is essential to be mindful of these cultural differences to avoid misunderstandings or causing offense.

Interpreting Eye Contact in Different Situations

The interpretation of eye contact can also vary depending on the context in which it occurs. Here are a few examples of how eye contact can be interpreted in different situations:

Job interviews: Maintaining good eye contact during a job interview is crucial as it demonstrates confidence, honesty, and interest in the position. It shows the interviewer that you are actively engaged and paying attention to what they are saying.

Social interactions: In social settings, eye contact is essential for building connections and establishing rapport. It shows that you are interested in the conversation and value the other person's presence. However, it is important to strike a balance and not make the other person feel uncomfortable by staring or maintaining intense eye contact for too long.

Public speaking: When giving a presentation or speaking in public, maintaining eye contact with the audience is vital. It helps to establish credibility, engage the listeners, and create a connection with them. Avoiding eye contact or constantly looking down can make you appear nervous or unprepared.

Romantic relationships: Eye contact plays a significant role in romantic relationships. Sustained eye contact can create a sense of intimacy and connection between partners. It can also be a way to communicate love, desire, or understanding without saying a word.

Improving Your Eye Contact Skills

If you struggle with maintaining eye contact or want to improve your eye contact skills, here are a few tips:

Practice: Start by practicing eye contact in low-pressure situations, such as with friends or family members. Gradually increase the duration of eye contact and work your way up to maintaining eye contact during more challenging conversations.

Be mindful of cultural differences: When interacting with individuals from different cultures, be aware of their cultural norms regarding eye contact. Adapt your behavior accordingly to show respect and avoid misunderstandings.

Pay attention to your body language: Eye contact is just one aspect of body language. Pay attention to your overall body language, such as your posture and facial expressions, to ensure that they align with your eye contact.

Take breaks: While maintaining eye contact is important, it is also essential to give yourself and the other person breaks. Avoid staring for too long, as it can make the other person feel uncomfortable. Take breaks by looking away briefly or focusing on other aspects of the conversation.

Making eye contact is a great way to communicate effectively. By understanding the different types of eye contact and their meanings, you can enhance your ability to read and interpret body language accurately. Practice and awareness will help you develop stronger connections with others and navigate social interactions more effectively.

Touch and Personal Space

Touch and personal space are important aspects of nonverbal communication that can convey a wide range of messages and emotions. The way we touch others and the distance we maintain from them can greatly influence our interactions and relationships. In this section, we will explore the significance of touch and personal space in body language and how to interpret these signals.

The Power of Touch

Touch is a powerful form of nonverbal communication that can convey various emotions, intentions, and meanings. From a gentle pat on the back to a firm handshake, touch can express warmth, support, affection, or even dominance. The meaning behind a touch can vary depending on the context, culture, and relationship between the individuals involved.

Types of Touch

Different types of touch can be observed in various situations:

Positive touch: This includes friendly gestures such as handshakes, hugs, and pats on the back. Positive touch can convey warmth, support, and a sense of connection.

Negative touch: Negative touch refers to aggressive or unwanted physical contact, such as pushing, hitting, or invading personal space. This touch type can indicate hostility, dominance, or a lack of respect.

Professional touch: In certain professional settings, such as healthcare or therapy, touch may be used to provide comfort or support. However, it is important to note that professional touch should always be appropriate, consensual, and within the boundaries of the professional relationship.

Cultural Differences in Touch

It is essential to consider cultural differences when interpreting touch in body language. Touch is viewed differently in different cultures, with differing expectations. For example, some cultures may embrace more physical contact, while others may have stricter boundaries. It is crucial to be aware of these cultural differences to avoid misunderstandings or discomfort.

Personal Space

The physical space we keep between ourselves and other people is referred to as personal space. The amount of personal space we require can vary depending on factors such as culture, individual preferences, and the nature of the relationship. Personal space is an important aspect of body language as it can influence our comfort levels and the dynamics of our interactions.

Zones of Personal Space

Edward T. Hall, an anthropologist distinguished four areas of personal space:

Intimate zone: This area, which varies in width from 0 to 18 inches, is designated for intimate partnerships, like those with family members or love partners. In this zone, touch is more likely to occur, and individuals may feel comfortable sharing personal information.

Personal zone: The personal zone extends from 18 inches to 4 feet and is typically maintained in casual social interactions. This distance allows for comfortable conversation and interaction without feeling too close or intrusive.

Social zone: The social zone spans from 4 to 12 feet and is common in formal or professional settings. This distance is appropriate for business meetings, presentations, or interactions with acquaintances.

Public zone: The public zone extends beyond 12 feet and is typically used in public spaces or large gatherings. In this zone, individuals maintain a greater physical distance, allowing for a sense of privacy and personal space.

Interpreting Personal Space

The distance individuals maintain in their interactions can provide valuable insights into their comfort levels, relationships, and intentions. Here are some general guidelines for interpreting personal space:

Proximity: When individuals stand or sit close to each other, it often indicates a close relationship or a desire for intimacy. This can be observed in romantic partners, close friends, or family members.

Comfortable distance: Maintaining a comfortable distance within the personal zone suggests a friendly and relaxed interaction. This is common in casual social settings or when individuals are getting to know each other.

Increased distance: If individuals maintain a greater distance, it may indicate a desire for more personal space or a lack of comfort. This can be observed when someone feels threatened, uncomfortable, or wants to establish a professional boundary.

Invasion of personal space: When someone invades another person's personal space without consent, it can be seen as intrusive or aggressive. This invasion can cause discomfort, anxiety, or a sense of violation.

Gender and Cultural Influences

It is important to note that gender and cultural influences can significantly impact touch and personal space. Different cultures may have different norms and expectations regarding touch, which can vary based on gender, age, and social status. For example, some cultures may have stricter boundaries for touch between unrelated individuals or between individuals of different genders.

Gender can play a role in the interpretation of touch and personal space. Society often imposes different expectations and norms on men and women regarding touch. For example, men may be expected to maintain a larger personal space and avoid certain types of touch, while women may be more socially permitted to engage in touch as a form of communication.

Understanding these gender and cultural influences is crucial to avoid misinterpretation and to respect the boundaries and comfort levels of others.

Touch and personal space are essential elements of nonverbal communication. The way we touch others and the distance we maintain can convey a wide range of emotions, intentions, and meanings. By understanding the power of touch and personal space and considering cultural and gender influences, we can better interpret these nonverbal signals and enhance our communication skills.

Chapter 3: Understanding Emotions through Body Language

Recognizing Happiness and Joy

Happiness and joy are two emotions that can be easily recognized through body language. When someone is genuinely happy or experiencing joy, their body language tends to be open, relaxed, and expressive.

Facial Expressions

Facial expressions are one of the most obvious indicators of happiness and joy. When someone is happy, their face will often light up with a genuine smile. A genuine smile involves the contraction of the muscles around the eyes, known as the Duchenne smile. This type of smile is difficult to fake and is a reliable indicator of true happiness.

Other facial expressions can also indicate happiness and joy. Raised eyebrows, a relaxed forehead, and a bright, lively look in the eyes are all signs of positive emotions. The overall expression of the face will appear relaxed and content.

Body Posture

The body posture of a person experiencing happiness or joy is usually open and relaxed. They may stand or sit upright with their shoulders back, displaying confidence and a positive attitude. Their movements will be fluid and energetic, reflecting their inner state of happiness.

When happy, they may also engage in playful and spontaneous movements. They may jump, dance, or skip, expressing their joy through their body language. Their gestures will be expansive and animated, reflecting their positive emotions.

Vocal Cues

Vocal cues can also provide valuable insights into someone's happiness and joy. When a person is genuinely happy, their voice will sound lively, energetic, and enthusiastic. They may speak with a higher pitch and a faster pace. Laughter is another vocal cue associated with happiness and joy. A genuine laugh is contagious and can instantly uplift the mood of those around.

Eye Contact

Eye contact plays a crucial role in conveying happiness and joy. When someone is happy, they will maintain good eye contact with others. Their eyes will appear bright and engaged, reflecting their positive emotions. They may also have a twinkle in their eyes, indicating their joy.

Gestures and Body Movements

Gestures and body movements can provide further clues about someone's happiness and joy. When someone is happy, they may engage in open and expansive gestures. They may use their hands to express themselves, making broad and sweeping movements. Their body movements will be fluid and relaxed, reflecting their positive emotions.

Energy and Enthusiasm

One of the key indicators of happiness and joy is the energy and enthusiasm displayed by an individual. When someone is genuinely happy, they will radiate positive energy and enthusiasm. They will be eager to engage with others, participate in activities, and share their joy with those around them. Their overall demeanor will be vibrant and lively.

Overall Demeanor

When someone is happy or experiencing joy, their overall demeanor will be upbeat. They will appear relaxed, content, and at ease. Their body language will exude confidence and positivity. They may also display a sense of gratitude and appreciation for the present moment.

Cultural Considerations

It is important to note that cultural differences can influence the expression of happiness and joy through body language. In some cultures, people may be more reserved in displaying their emotions, while in others, they may be more expressive. It is essential to consider cultural norms and individual differences when interpreting body language cues related to happiness and joy.

Recognizing happiness and joy through body language involves observing facial expressions, body posture, vocal cues, eye contact, gestures, energy levels, and overall demeanor. By paying attention to these nonverbal cues, you can gain valuable insights into someone's emotional state and connect with them on a deeper level.

Identifying Sadness and Grief

Sadness and grief are universal emotions that can be easily recognized through body language cues. When someone is experiencing sadness or grief, their body language often reflects their emotional state. By understanding and interpreting these nonverbal signals, you can gain insight into a person's emotional well-being and offer support when needed.

Facial Expressions

Facial expressions are one of the most noticeable indicators of sadness and grief. When someone is feeling sad or grieving, their facial muscles may appear tense or droopy. The corners of their mouth may be turned downward, and their eyebrows may be furrowed. Their eyes may appear watery or red, and they may avoid making direct eye contact.

Posture

The posture of someone experiencing sadness or grief may also change. They may slouch or hunch their shoulders as if carrying a heavy burden. Their body may appear tense, and they may have a lack of energy or motivation. In some cases, individuals may curl up into a fetal position, seeking comfort and protection.

Gestures

Gestures can also provide valuable insights into a person's emotional state. When someone is sad or grieving, they may engage in self-soothing behaviors such as hugging themselves or crossing their arms tightly across their chest.

They may also exhibit slower and more deliberate movements as if weighed down by their emotions.

Vocal Cues

Vocal cues can also indicate sadness and grief. When someone is feeling sad, their voice may become softer and more monotone. They may speak at a slower pace and use fewer words. In some cases, individuals may also experience a catch in their voice or struggle to speak due to the intensity of their emotions.

Withdrawal

Sadness and grief can often lead to social withdrawal. Individuals may isolate themselves from others, seeking solitude to process their emotions. They might steer clear of social events or abruptly cancel scheduled activities. When interacting with others, they may appear distant or disengaged, as their thoughts are consumed by their sadness or grief.

Changes in Appetite and Sleep Patterns

Sadness and grief can also impact a person's appetite and sleep patterns. Some individuals may experience a loss of appetite and have difficulty eating, while others may turn to food as a source of comfort and overeat. Similarly, sleep patterns may be disrupted, with individuals experiencing difficulty falling asleep or staying asleep throughout the night.

Emotional Outbursts

While sadness and grief are often associated with a subdued emotional state, individuals may also experience emotional outbursts. These outbursts can manifest as crying spells, anger, or irritability. It is important to remember that these outbursts are a normal part of the grieving process and should be met with empathy and understanding.

Providing Support

When identifying sadness and grief in others, it is essential to approach the situation with empathy and compassion. Here are a few ways you can offer assistance:

Active Listening: Give the person your full attention and listen without judgment. Allow them to express their emotions and thoughts without interruption.

Validate Their Feelings: Let the person know that their feelings are valid and that it is okay to grieve. Refrain from downplaying their feelings or giving them unsolicited advice.

Offer Comfort: Provide physical comfort through a gentle touch or a hug, if appropriate and welcomed. Sometimes, a simple gesture of support can go a long way.

Be Patient: Grief takes time, and everyone processes emotions differently. Be patient with the person and allow them to grieve at their own pace.

Encourage Self-Care: Remind the person to take care of themselves physically, emotionally, and mentally. Encourage them to engage in activities that bring them comfort and joy.

Seek Professional Help: If the person's sadness or grief becomes overwhelming or prolonged, encourage them to seek professional help from a therapist or counselor who specializes in grief counseling.

Understanding and identifying sadness and grief through body language can help you provide the necessary support and empathy to those who are experiencing these emotions. By being attentive to nonverbal cues and offering a compassionate presence, you can make a positive difference in someone's life during their time of need.

Detecting Anger and Frustration

Anger and frustration are powerful emotions that can be easily conveyed through body language. Being able to detect these emotions in others can help you navigate difficult situations and respond appropriately

Facial Expressions

Facial expressions are one of the most noticeable and reliable indicators of anger and frustration. When someone is angry or frustrated, their facial muscles may tense up, and their expressions may become more intense. Look for the following cues:

Furrowed brows: When someone is angry or frustrated, they may furrow their brows, creating vertical lines between their eyebrows. This is a clear sign of tension and displeasure.

Tightened jaw: Anger and frustration can cause individuals to clench their jaw tightly. This can be observed through a visible tightening of the jaw muscles or even grinding of the teeth.

Flared nostrils: When someone is angry, their nostrils may flare as they take in more air to fuel their heightened emotions.

Intense gaze: Angry individuals often have an intense and piercing gaze. Their eyes may narrow, and they may maintain strong eye contact as a way to assert dominance or convey their displeasure.

Body Posture

The way a person carries can also provide valuable insights into their anger or frustration. Keep an eye out for the following signs of body language:

Tense muscles: When someone is angry or frustrated, their muscles may become tense and rigid. They may stand or sit with a stiff posture, indicating their heightened emotional state.

Aggressive gestures: Anger can manifest in gestures such as clenched fists, pointing fingers, or pounding on surfaces. These gestures are a clear indication of frustration and anger.

Pacing or fidgeting: When someone is angry or frustrated, they may have difficulty staying still. They may pace back and forth, tap their fingers, or engage in other restless movements as a way to release their pent-up energy.

Invasion of personal space: Anger can lead individuals to invade the personal space of others as a way to assert dominance or intimidate. They may stand too close, lean in aggressively, or invade the personal boundaries of others.

Vocal Cues

Vocal cues can also provide valuable information about someone's anger or frustration. Pay attention to the following vocal cues:

Raised voice: When someone is angry or frustrated, their voice may become louder and more forceful. They may shout or speak with an aggressive tone as a way to express their emotions.

Rapid speech: Anger can cause individuals to speak quickly and with a sense of urgency. Their words may be delivered in a rapid-fire manner, reflecting their heightened emotional state.

Sarcastic or biting tone: Frustration can lead to the use of sarcasm or a biting tone. The individual may make cutting remarks or use passive-aggressive language to express their displeasure.

Microexpressions

Microexpressions are quick changes in facial expression that happen in milliseconds. They can provide valuable insights into someone's true emotions, including anger and frustration. Look for the following microexpressions:

Brow furrow: A quick furrowing of the brows can indicate anger or frustration.

Lip compression: A brief compression or tightening of the lips can be a sign of suppressed anger.

Jaw clench: A momentary clenching of the jaw can indicate frustration or anger.

Other Indicators

Other indicators can help you detect anger and frustration in body language:

Increased perspiration: When someone is angry or frustrated, their body may produce more sweat as a physiological response to their heightened emotions.

Redness in the face: Anger can cause increased blood flow to the face, resulting in a reddening of the skin.

Agitated movements: Anger and frustration can lead to restless movements such as pacing, tapping, or fidgeting.

By paying attention to these nonverbal cues, you can become more adept at detecting anger and frustration in others. However, it is important to remember that body language is not always a definitive indicator of someone's emotions. It is essential to consider the context and other factors before making any assumptions.

Interpreting Fear and Anxiety

Fear and anxiety are two powerful emotions that can be easily detected through body language. When someone is afraid or anxious, their body undergoes various changes that can give away their true feelings. Understanding how to interpret these signals can help you better understand and empathize with others, as well as navigate potentially challenging situations.

Facial Expressions of Fear and Anxiety

The face is one of the most expressive parts of the body, and it can reveal a lot about a person's emotional state. When someone is experiencing fear or anxiety, their facial expressions may display certain telltale signs. These can include:

Wide eyes: When someone is afraid or anxious, their eyes may widen as they try to take in as much information as possible. This can also be accompanied by raised eyebrows.

Tense jaw: Fear and anxiety can cause the jaw muscles to tighten, leading to a clenched or gritted teeth appearance.

Furrowed brow: A furrowed brow is a common sign of worry or concern. When someone is afraid or anxious, they may unconsciously furrow their brow as a way to protect themselves.

Lip biting or licking: Nervousness can manifest in the form of lip biting or licking. This can be a subconscious attempt to soothe oneself or a sign of inner tension.

Rapid breathing: Fear and anxiety can cause an increase in breathing rate. Look for shallow, rapid breaths or visible signs of heavy breathing.

Body Posture and Movements

Body posture and movements can also provide valuable insights into a person's fear or anxiety. Among the typical body language cues to be aware of are:

Tense muscles: When someone is afraid or anxious, their muscles may become tense and rigid. This can be seen in their posture, with their shoulders hunched and body leaning forward or backward.

Restlessness: Fear and anxiety can make a person feel restless and fidgety. They may constantly shift their weight from one foot to another, tap their fingers, or pace back and forth.

Defensive gestures: When feeling threatened, people may instinctively adopt defensive gestures. This can include crossing their arms, hugging themselves, or placing objects in front of their body as a form of protection.

Avoidance of eye contact: Fear and anxiety can make it difficult for someone to maintain eye contact. They may look away or down, avoiding direct gaze as a way to protect themselves or hide their true emotions.

Freezing or immobility: In some cases, fear or anxiety can cause a person to freeze or become immobile. This can be seen as a sudden stillness or lack of movement as if they are trying to blend into their surroundings or avoid drawing attention to themselves.

Vocal Cues

While body language is primarily nonverbal, vocal cues can also provide valuable information about a person's fear or anxiety. Pay attention to the following vocal cues:

Trembling voice: Fear and anxiety can cause a person's voice to tremble or shake. This can be a result of increased muscle tension or heightened emotions.

Quivering or shaky breaths: When someone is afraid or anxious, their breath may become shallow and unsteady. This can manifest as quivering or shaky breaths, which can be audible or visible.

Increased speech rate: Fear and anxiety can cause a person to speak more quickly than usual. They may rush their words or stumble over their sentences as their thoughts race.

Soft or weak voice: Some individuals may experience a decrease in vocal volume when they are afraid or anxious. Their voice may become softer or weaker as they try to minimize their presence or avoid drawing attention to themselves.

Clusters of Signals

Interpreting body language is not about relying on a single signal but rather looking for clusters of signals. A single gesture or expression may not always accurately reflect a person's emotional state. By observing multiple signals that align with fear or anxiety, you can have a more accurate understanding of what someone is experiencing.

It's crucial to consider individual differences and cultural norms when interpreting body language. Not everyone displays fear or anxiety in the same way, and cultural backgrounds can influence how emotions are expressed. It's essential to approach body language interpretation with sensitivity and open-mindedness.

By learning to interpret the body language signals associated with fear and anxiety, you can develop a deeper understanding of others and enhance your communication skills. This knowledge can be particularly valuable in situations where empathy and support are needed, such as during times of distress or when helping someone overcome their fears.

Decoding Disgust and Contempt

In body language, certain emotions can be quite challenging to decipher. Disgust and contempt are two such emotions that can be subtle yet powerful in their expression. Understanding how to decode these emotions through body language can provide valuable insights into a person's thoughts and feelings.

Recognizing Disgust

Disgust is an emotion that is often associated with a feeling of revulsion or aversion towards something unpleasant or offensive. When someone experiences disgust, their body language can provide clues to their emotional state. The following are some crucial signs to watch out for:

Facial Expressions: The face is a primary source of nonverbal cues, and it plays a significant role in expressing disgust. Look for wrinkling of the nose, raised upper lip, and a downward pull of the corners of the mouth. These facial expressions are often accompanied by a squinting of the eyes and a furrowing of the brow.

Body Movements: Disgust can also be reflected in certain body movements. People may exhibit a recoiling or pulling away motion as if trying to physically distance themselves from the source of their disgust. They may also cross their arms or legs, creating a barrier between themselves and the object or situation that elicits the feeling of disgust.

Verbal Cues: Pay attention to the words and tone of voice used by the person displaying disgust. They may use words or phrases that convey a sense of repulsion or distaste. Their tone of voice may be sharp or condescending, emphasizing their negative feelings towards the subject at hand.

Microexpressions: Microexpressions are quick changes in facial expression that happen in milliseconds. When someone experiences disgust, you may observe a quick, subtle expression of disgust that flashes across their face before they regain control of their emotions. These microexpressions can be challenging to detect, but with practice, you can become more adept at recognizing them.

Interpreting Contempt

Contempt is an emotion that is characterized by a feeling of superiority or disdain towards someone or something. It often involves a sense of moral or intellectual superiority. Decoding contempt through body language can be particularly useful in understanding power dynamics and interpersonal relationships. The following are important signs to watch out for:

Facial Expressions: Contempt is often displayed through subtle facial expressions. Look for a slight curling of the lip on one side of the mouth, accompanied by a raised eyebrow on the same side. This asymmetrical expression is a telltale sign of contempt. The person may also have a smug or self-satisfied expression on their face.

Eye Movements: When someone feels contempt, they may engage in eye-rolling or a dismissive gaze. They may look away or avoid direct eye contact with the person or object of their contempt. This behavior signifies a lack of interest or respect.

Body Posture: Contempt can be reflected in the way a person carries. They may adopt a relaxed or nonchalant posture, leaning back or casually crossing their legs. This posture conveys a sense of superiority and indifference towards others.

Verbal Cues: Pay attention to the words and tone of voice used by the person displaying contempt. They may use sarcastic or mocking language, belittling others or their ideas. Their tone of voice may be condescending or patronizing, emphasizing their sense of superiority.

Microexpressions: Similar to disgust, contempt can also be expressed through microexpressions. These fleeting expressions may include a subtle sneer or a tightening of the lips. They can provide valuable insights into a person's true feelings, even when they are trying to mask their contempt.

Context and Cultural Considerations

It is important to note that the interpretation of body language, including disgust and contempt, should always be done in the context of the situation and the individual's cultural background. Different cultures may have varying norms and expressions for these emotions. What may be considered a sign of disgust or contempt in one culture may have a different meaning in another.

It is crucial to consider the overall context in which the body language is being displayed. A person may exhibit signs of disgust or contempt towards a specific object or situation, but it does not necessarily mean that they feel the same way

75

towards everything or everyone. It is essential to look for consistency in their body language and consider other nonverbal cues to gain a more accurate understanding of their emotions.

Decoding emotions such as disgust and contempt through body language can provide valuable insights into a person's thoughts and feelings. By paying attention to facial expressions, body movements, verbal cues, and microexpressions, you can gain a deeper understanding of these complex emotions.

It is important to consider the context and cultural background of the individual to avoid misinterpretation. With practice and observation, you can become more proficient in reading and understanding body language, enhancing your communication skills and interpersonal relationships.

Spotting Surprise and Confusion

Surprise and confusion are two emotions that can be easily detected through body language. In this section, we will explore the various nonverbal cues that indicate surprise and confusion, and how to accurately interpret them.

Surprise

Surprise is a sudden and unexpected reaction to something. It can be positive or negative, depending on the context. When someone is surprised, their body language often reflects their emotional state. Here are some common nonverbal cues that indicate surprise:

Facial Expressions: The eyebrows are raised, and the eyes widen. The mouth may open slightly, and the jaw may drop. These facial expressions are universal and can be observed across different cultures.

Body Movements: The body may tense up momentarily, and the person may lean forward or backward in response to the surprise. There may also be a quick, involuntary movement, such as a jump or a startle.

Gestures: Surprise can be expressed through gestures such as covering the mouth with a hand or placing a hand on the chest. These gestures are instinctive and serve to protect oneself or show vulnerability.

Vocal Cues: A surprised person may gasp, exclaim, or make a sudden sound. The tone of their voice may also change, becoming higher or louder.

Eye Contact: When surprised, people tend to widen their eyes and maintain eye contact with the source of the surprise. They may also look around in search of further information or clarification.

It is important to note that surprise can be fleeting, and the body language associated with it may only last for a brief moment. Therefore, it is crucial to pay close attention to these cues as they occur.

Confusion

Confusion is a state of uncertainty or lack of understanding. It can arise when someone is faced with complex or contradictory information. Detecting confusion through body language can help you gauge whether someone is struggling to comprehend or process what is being communicated. Here are some common nonverbal cues that indicate confusion:

Facial Expressions: The person may furrow their brow, creating vertical lines between their eyebrows. They may also tilt their head to the side or squint their eyes in an attempt to understand better.

Body Movements: Confusion can be expressed through body movements such as scratching the head, rubbing the temples, or touching the face. These actions indicate a person's attempt to stimulate their thinking or alleviate mental stress.

Gestures: The person may use gestures that indicate uncertainty, such as shrugging their shoulders or spreading their hands apart in a questioning manner. These gestures convey a lack of clarity or understanding.

Vocal Cues: Confusion can be reflected in the tone of voice. The person may speak hesitantly, pause frequently, or use filler words such as "um" or "uh" as they search for the right words or try to gather their thoughts.

Body Posture: A confused person may adopt a closed-off posture, crossing their arms or hunching their shoulders.

They may also exhibit restless movements, such as fidgeting or shifting their weight from one foot to another.

When interpreting confusion, it is essential to consider the context and the individual's baseline behavior. Some people naturally display more confusion in their body language, while others may mask it. Therefore, it is crucial to look for clusters of cues and compare them to the person's usual behavior to accurately assess their level of confusion.

Spotting surprise and confusion through body language can provide valuable insights into a person's emotional state and level of understanding. By paying attention to facial expressions, body movements, gestures, vocal cues, and body posture, you can better understand and empathize with others.

Body language is just one piece of the puzzle, and it should be considered in conjunction with verbal communication and other contextual factors. Developing your ability to read and interpret body language will enhance your overall communication skills and enable you to navigate social interactions more effectively.

Chapter 4: Body Language in Different Contexts

Body Language in Social Interactions

Our everyday lives revolve around social interactions. Whether we are meeting new people, catching up with friends, or engaging in group activities, understanding body language can greatly enhance our communication skills and help us navigate social situations more effectively.

The Importance of Body Language in Social Interactions

Body language plays a crucial role in social interactions as it often conveys more information than verbal communication alone. It helps us understand the emotions, intentions, and attitudes of others, allowing us to respond appropriately and build stronger connections. By paying attention to nonverbal cues, we can gain valuable insights into a person's thoughts and feelings, even when they are not explicitly expressed.

Facial Expressions and Microexpressions

One of the most effective nonverbal communication tools is facial expression. They can convey a wide range of emotions, including happiness, sadness, anger, surprise, and disgust. By observing someone's facial expressions, we can gauge their emotional state and adjust our behavior accordingly.

Microexpressions, on the other hand, are fleeting facial expressions that occur within a fraction of a second. They often reveal true emotions that people may try to conceal. Learning to recognize microexpressions can provide valuable insights into someone's true feelings, helping us to better understand their intentions and motivations.

Gestures and Posture

Gestures and posture also play a significant role in social interactions. They can convey confidence, openness, and engagement, or conversely, insecurity, defensiveness, and disinterest. Paying attention to someone's gestures and posture can help us assess their level of comfort, engagement, and receptiveness in a conversation.

For example, crossed arms and a closed-off posture may indicate defensiveness or disagreement, while open arms and an upright posture may suggest openness and attentiveness. Similarly, hand gestures can provide additional context to verbal communication, emphasizing certain points or conveying emotions.

Eye Contact and Gaze

Eye contact is a powerful form of nonverbal communication that can establish trust, convey interest, and facilitate connection. Maintaining appropriate eye contact during a conversation signals attentiveness and engagement. It is important to note that cultural norms and personal preferences can influence eye contact patterns, so it is essential to be mindful of individual differences.

Gaze direction is another important aspect of body language. People tend to look at what they find interesting or important. By observing someone's gaze, we can gain insights into their focus of attention and their level of interest in a particular topic or person.

Proxemics and Personal Space

Proxemics refers to the study of personal space and the distance we maintain between ourselves and others during social interactions. Different cultures have varying norms regarding personal space, and violating these norms can lead to discomfort or misinterpretation.

Understanding proxemics can help us navigate social interactions more effectively. For example, standing too close to someone may be perceived as intrusive or aggressive, while standing too far away may convey disinterest or aloofness. By respecting personal space boundaries, we can create a more comfortable and respectful environment for social interactions.

Vocal Cues and Tone of Voice

While body language primarily focuses on nonverbal cues, vocal cues and tone of voice also play a significant role in social interactions. Our speech patterns, which include intonation, loudness, and pitch, can express attitudes, feelings, and intentions.

For instance, a soft and soothing tone of voice may indicate empathy or comfort, while a loud and aggressive tone may convey anger or frustration. By paying attention to vocal cues, we can gain a deeper understanding of someone's emotional state and respond accordingly.

Cultural Considerations

It's crucial to remember that body language signals can differ depending on the culture. Gestures, facial expressions, and personal space norms may have different meanings or interpretations in various cultural contexts. Therefore, it is crucial to be aware of these cultural differences and adapt our understanding of body language accordingly when interacting with individuals from different backgrounds.

Practicing Observation and Awareness

To become proficient in reading body language in social interactions, it is essential to practice observation and develop self-awareness. Paying attention to the nonverbal cues of others and reflecting on our body language can help us become more attuned to the subtleties of communication.

By actively observing and analyzing body language in various social settings, we can improve our ability to interpret nonverbal cues accurately. Being aware of our body language allows us to make conscious adjustments to convey our intentions and emotions more effectively.

Body language plays a vital role in social interactions. By understanding and interpreting nonverbal cues, we can enhance our communication skills, build stronger connections, and navigate social situations with greater ease. By practicing observation, awareness, and cultural sensitivity, we can become more proficient in reading body language and effectively communicate with others.

Body Language in the Workplace

Body language plays a crucial role in the workplace, as it can greatly impact how others perceive us and how we communicate with our colleagues. Understanding and interpreting body language in the workplace can help us navigate professional relationships, enhance communication, and improve overall workplace dynamics. In this section, we will explore the various aspects of body language in the workplace and provide practical tips on how to effectively read and respond to nonverbal cues.

Establishing Rapport and Building Trust

Building rapport and establishing trust are essential in any workplace setting. Body language can play a significant role in creating a positive and trustworthy impression. When engaging in conversations with colleagues or superiors, it is important to maintain open and welcoming body language. This includes maintaining eye contact, nodding to show understanding and interest, and using appropriate facial expressions to convey attentiveness and engagement.

Mirroring or matching the body language of others can help establish rapport. Mirroring involves subtly imitating the body language of the person you are interacting with, such as their posture, gestures, or facial expressions. This technique can create a sense of familiarity and connection, making the other person feel more comfortable and at ease.

Interpreting Power Dynamics

Body language can also provide valuable insights into power dynamics within the workplace. In hierarchical settings, individuals in positions of authority often display dominant body language cues, such as standing tall, using expansive gestures, and maintaining strong eye contact. On the other hand, individuals in subordinate positions may exhibit more submissive body language, such as avoiding direct eye contact, slouching, or using smaller gestures.

Understanding these power dynamics can help us navigate workplace interactions more effectively. For example, if we are in a subordinate position, it is important to be mindful of our body language and ensure that it conveys respect and professionalism. Conversely, if we are in a position of authority, we should be aware of how our body language may be perceived by others and strive to create an inclusive and approachable environment.

Nonverbal Communication in Meetings and Presentations

Meetings and presentations are common in the workplace, and nonverbal cues can greatly impact the effectiveness of these interactions. When presenting or speaking in a meeting, it is important to maintain confident and assertive body language. This includes standing tall, using open gestures, and maintaining eye contact with the audience.

Being aware of the nonverbal cues of others in meetings can provide valuable insights into their engagement and understanding. For example, crossed arms or a lack of eye contact may indicate disinterest or disagreement, while leaning forward and nodding can signal attentiveness and agreement. By paying attention to these cues, we can adjust our communication style and ensure that our message is effectively received.

Managing Conflict and Difficult Conversations

Conflict and difficult conversations are inevitable in the workplace, and understanding body language can help navigate these situations more effectively. When engaged in a conflict or difficult conversation, it is important to remain calm and composed. This can be conveyed through open body language, such as uncrossed arms, relaxed posture, and maintaining eye contact.

Active listening is also crucial in these situations. By using appropriate nonverbal cues, such as nodding, maintaining eye contact, and leaning forward, we can demonstrate our attentiveness and show that we value the other person's perspective. Avoiding defensive body language, such as crossing arms or avoiding eye contact, can help create a more open and productive dialogue.

Cultural Sensitivity in Body Language

In today's diverse workplaces, it is important to be mindful of cultural differences in body language. Different cultures may have varying norms and interpretations of nonverbal cues. For example, direct eye contact may be seen as a sign of respect in some cultures, while in others, it may be considered disrespectful or confrontational.

To navigate these cultural differences, it is important to educate ourselves about the cultural norms of our colleagues and clients. Being respectful and adaptable in our body language can help foster positive relationships and avoid misunderstandings. When in doubt, it is always best to err on the side of caution and observe the body language cues of others before adjusting our own.

Understanding and interpreting body language in the workplace is a valuable skill that can enhance communication, build rapport, and improve overall workplace dynamics. By being aware of our body language and paying attention to the nonverbal cues of others, we can navigate professional relationships more effectively and create a positive and inclusive work environment.

Body Language in Romantic Relationships

Romantic relationships are built on a foundation of trust, understanding, and effective communication. While verbal communication plays a crucial role in expressing emotions and thoughts, body language also plays a significant part in conveying messages in a romantic relationship. Understanding and interpreting body language in this context can help deepen the connection between partners, enhance intimacy, and resolve conflicts more effectively.

The Power of Touch

Touch is a powerful form of nonverbal communication that can convey a wide range of emotions and intentions in a romantic relationship. It can express love, affection, comfort, and desire. The way partners touch each other can reveal their level of intimacy and connection. For example, gentle caresses, holding hands, and hugging can indicate a strong emotional bond and a desire for closeness. On the other hand, a lack of physical touch or avoidance of touch may suggest emotional distance or discomfort.

It is important to note that the meaning of touch can vary between individuals and cultures. Some people may have different comfort levels with physical touch, and it is essential to respect each other's boundaries and preferences. Open and honest communication about touch can help partners understand each other's needs and ensure that both feel comfortable and respected.

Facial Expressions and Eye Contact

Facial expressions are one of the most powerful ways to convey emotions and intentions. In a romantic relationship, partners often rely on facial expressions to understand each other's feelings and desires. A genuine smile can indicate happiness and contentment, while a furrowed brow or a frown may suggest concern or sadness.

Eye contact is another crucial aspect of body language in romantic relationships. Maintaining eye contact during conversations shows attentiveness and interest. It can create a sense of connection and intimacy between partners. However, prolonged or intense eye contact can also be interpreted as a sign of aggression or dominance. It is important to find a balance and be aware of cultural differences in eye contact norms.

Posture and Body Alignment

Posture and body alignment can reveal a lot about a person's emotional state and level of comfort in a romantic relationship. When partners feel relaxed and at ease with each other, their bodies tend to be more open and aligned. They may lean towards each other, face each other directly, and have a relaxed posture. This indicates a sense of trust and engagement.

On the other hand, crossed arms turned-away bodies, or a tense posture can suggest defensiveness, discomfort, or a lack of interest. It is important to pay attention to these nonverbal cues and address any underlying issues that may be causing tension or disconnection.

Nonverbal Communication During Conflict

Conflict is a natural part of any relationship, including romantic ones. During conflicts, body language can either escalate or de-escalate the situation. It is important to be aware of nonverbal cues that may indicate anger, frustration, or defensiveness. These can include clenched fists, raised voices, crossed arms, or a rigid posture.

To effectively navigate conflicts, it is crucial to practice active listening and open body language. This involves maintaining eye contact, facing each other directly, and using open gestures. It is also important to regulate emotions and avoid aggressive or defensive body language, such as pointing fingers or invading personal space. By being mindful of nonverbal cues during conflicts, partners can create a safe and respectful environment for open communication and problem-solving.

Building Intimacy through Body Language

Body language plays a significant role in building intimacy and connection in romantic relationships. It can enhance emotional and physical intimacy by creating a sense of safety, trust, and understanding. Here are some ways partners can use body language to strengthen their bond:

Active Listening: Show interest and attentiveness by maintaining eye contact, nodding, and using affirmative gestures. This conveys that you value and respect your partner's thoughts and feelings.

Physical Affection: Express love and affection through gentle touches, hugs, and kisses. Physical affection releases oxytocin, a hormone that promotes bonding and intimacy.

Mirroring: Mirroring your partner's body language can create a sense of connection and understanding. Subtly imitating their gestures, posture, and facial expressions can help establish rapport and empathy.

Shared Activities: Engaging in activities together that require physical closeness, such as dancing or cooking, can strengthen the bond between partners and create shared experiences.

Nonverbal Reassurance: During moments of vulnerability or distress, nonverbal cues such as holding hands, offering a comforting touch, or maintaining close physical proximity can provide reassurance and support.

By being mindful of these nonverbal cues and actively incorporating them into their relationship, partners can deepen their emotional connection and create a more fulfilling and intimate bond.

Body language plays a vital role in romantic relationships, allowing partners to communicate and understand each other on a deeper level. By paying attention to nonverbal cues such as touch, facial expressions, eye contact, posture, and body alignment, partners can enhance their emotional connection, resolve conflicts more effectively, and build a stronger and more intimate bond. Understanding and interpreting body language in a romantic relationship requires open communication, respect for boundaries, and a willingness to be attentive and responsive to each other's needs.

Body Language in Public Speaking

Many people find public speaking to be an extremely nerve-wracking experience. The pressure of standing in front of a crowd and delivering a speech can cause anxiety and stress. Understanding and utilizing body language can greatly enhance your public speaking skills and help you connect with your audience on a deeper level.

The Importance of Body Language in Public Speaking

Body language plays a crucial role in public speaking as it can convey your confidence, credibility, and authenticity to the audience. It is estimated that more than half of our communication is nonverbal, and this includes the way we use our bodies to express ourselves. When you are speaking in front of a crowd, your body language can either enhance or detract from your message.

Projecting Confidence

When it comes to public speaking, confidence is essential. Your body language can either project confidence or reveal your nervousness. To appear confident, stand tall with your shoulders back and your head held high. Avoid slouching or crossing your arms, as these gestures can make you appear closed off and insecure.

Maintain good eye contact with your audience to establish a connection and show that you are engaged with them. Avoid looking down or focusing on one spot for too long. Instead, scan the room and make eye contact with different individuals throughout your speech.

Using Gestures Effectively

Gestures can be a powerful tool in public speaking as they can help emphasize your points and make your speech more engaging. It is important to use gestures naturally and purposefully. Avoid excessive or random movements that can distract your audience.

Use your hands to illustrate your ideas and create visual imagery. For example, if you are talking about the size of something, you can use your hands to show the dimensions. Be mindful of the size and speed of your gestures, as exaggerated or fast movements can be overwhelming for the audience.

Facial Expressions and Vocal Variety

Your facial expressions can convey a range of emotions and greatly impact how your message is received. Smile genuinely to create a positive and welcoming atmosphere. Show enthusiasm and passion through your facial expressions to captivate your audience.

Vocal variety is another important aspect of public speaking. Vary your tone, pitch, and volume to add emphasis and keep your audience engaged. Use pauses strategically to allow your audience to absorb your message and create anticipation.

Body Language and Audience Engagement

Engaging your audience is crucial for a successful public speaking experience. Your body language can help create a connection and keep your audience interested throughout your speech. Here are some tips for using body language to engage your audience:

Move around the stage: Avoid standing in one spot for the entire duration of your speech. Move around the stage to create visual interest and show your energy.

Use open and inviting gestures: Open gestures, such as open palms and outstretched arms, can make you appear approachable and friendly. Use these gestures to invite your audience to connect with you.

Mirror your audience: Mirroring is a technique where you subtly mimic the body language of your audience. This can create a sense of rapport and make your audience feel more connected to you.

Pay attention to your posture: Stand tall and maintain good posture throughout your speech. This not only conveys confidence but also allows your voice to project better.

Managing Nervousness

Even the most experienced public speakers can experience nervousness before and during a speech. By understanding and managing your body language, you can effectively control your nerves and appear more confident.

One technique to manage nervousness is deep breathing. Take slow, deep breaths before and during your speech to calm your nerves and regulate your body's stress response. This will help you maintain a steady and controlled body language.

Another technique is visualization. Before you speak, picture yourself giving an interesting and successful presentation. Imagine yourself using confident body language and receiving positive feedback from your audience. You can feel less anxious and more confident after using this mental practice.

Body language plays a vital role in public speaking. By understanding and utilizing effective body language techniques, you can enhance your communication skills, connect with your audience, and deliver a powerful and memorable speech. Always project confidence, use gestures purposefully, and engage your audience through your body language. With practice and awareness, you can become a master of body language in public speaking.

Chapter 5: Detecting Deception through Body Language

Signs of Lying

When it comes to detecting deception, understanding the signs of lying can be a valuable skill. While it is important to note that no single body language cue can definitively indicate that someone is lying, several common behaviors may suggest deception. By being aware of these signs, you can become more adept at reading body language and identifying potential lies.

Facial Expressions

Facial expressions can provide valuable clues when trying to determine if someone is lying. While it is essential to consider individual differences and cultural norms, there are some general signs to look out for:

Microexpressions: These are brief, involuntary facial expressions that occur when a person tries to conceal their true emotions. They typically last for only a fraction of a second and can reveal underlying emotions that contradict what the person is saying.

Lack of eye contact: Avoiding eye contact or looking away frequently can be a sign of deception. However, it is important to note that some individuals may naturally avoid eye contact due to shyness or cultural differences, so it is crucial to consider other cues as well.

Covering the mouth or face: People may instinctively cover their mouth or face when they are lying to subconsciously block the deceitful words from escaping. This gesture can be a sign of discomfort or an attempt to hide something.

Excessive blinking: Rapid blinking or an increase in the frequency of blinking can indicate nervousness or anxiety, which may be associated with lying. However, it is essential to consider the person's baseline behavior and any potential medical conditions that may affect their blinking patterns.

Body Movements and Gestures

Body movements and gestures can also provide valuable insights into whether someone is lying. Observe the following typical indicators:

Fidgeting: When people are lying, they may exhibit increased fidgeting or restlessness. This can include tapping their fingers, shaking their legs, or constantly shifting their weight from one foot to another. These movements can be a result of nervousness or discomfort.

Closed-off body language: Liars may subconsciously try to create a physical barrier between themselves and the person they are deceiving. They may cross their arms, hunch their shoulders, or create distance by leaning away. These defensive postures can be a sign that they are trying to protect themselves from being caught in a lie.

Inconsistent gestures: When someone is lying, their body language may not align with their words. For example, they may nod their head in agreement while saying something contradictory or display gestures that do not match the emotions they are expressing. These inconsistencies can be indicative of deception.

Exaggerated or forced gestures: Liars may overcompensate by using exaggerated or forced gestures to appear more convincing. These gestures may seem unnatural or out of sync with their overall body language and can be a sign that they are trying too hard to deceive.

Verbal Cues

While body language plays a significant role in detecting deception, it is essential to consider verbal cues as well. Pay attention to the following signs when trying to determine if someone is lying:

Inconsistencies in speech: Liars may struggle to maintain consistency in their story. They may contradict themselves, provide vague or evasive answers, or offer excessive details to divert attention from the truth. Inconsistencies in their verbal responses can be a strong indicator of deception.

Changes in vocal tone: When people lie, their vocal tone may change. They may speak in a higher pitch, sound more hesitant, or exhibit signs of nervousness such as stuttering or stammering. These changes can be a result of the anxiety associated with lying.

Avoidance of direct answers: Liars may try to avoid answering direct questions by deflecting or changing the subject. They may also respond with evasive language or provide vague explanations. These tactics can be an attempt to divert attention from the truth and maintain deception.

Overemphasis on certain details: Liars may overemphasize certain details or provide excessive information to make their story appear more believable. By focusing on specific aspects, they hope to distract from the overall deception. Pay attention to whether the person seems overly concerned with convincing you of their honesty.

These signs of lying are not foolproof and should be considered in conjunction with other factors. It is crucial to establish a baseline of the person's normal behavior and take into account individual differences and cultural norms. It is essential to approach the detection of deception with empathy and understanding, as there may be underlying reasons why someone chooses to lie.

Microexpressions and Deceptive Behaviors

Microexpressions are brief, involuntary facial expressions that occur in response to a person's emotions. They are often fleeting and can be difficult to detect, but they can provide valuable insights into a person's true feelings and intentions. In the context of body language, microexpressions are particularly important when it comes to detecting deception.

Understanding Microexpressions

Microexpressions are universal and occur across cultures, making them a reliable indicator of a person's true emotions. They typically last for only a fraction of a second, but they can reveal a person's true feelings even when they are trying to conceal them. These microexpressions are often subconscious and occur before a person has a chance to consciously control their facial expressions.

Seven universal microexpressions have been identified by psychologist Paul Ekman: happiness, sadness, anger, fear, surprise, disgust, and contempt. Each of these microexpressions is associated with specific facial muscle movements that can be observed and interpreted.

Detecting Deceptive Behaviors

Deception is a complex behavior that involves intentionally misleading others. When people lie, they often try to control their facial expressions to appear genuine. Microexpressions can reveal their true emotions and intentions, providing clues to their deception.

When someone is being deceptive, they may display microexpressions that are incongruent with their verbal statements or other nonverbal cues. For example, a person who is lying about being happy may display a microexpression of sadness or fear. These incongruences can be subtle and fleeting, but they can be detected with careful observation.

Recognizing Microexpressions

Detecting microexpressions requires keen observation skills and practice. Here are some tips to help you recognize microexpressions and deceptive behaviors:

Pay attention to the timing: Microexpressions occur very quickly, so it's important to be attentive and focused. Train yourself to observe people's faces closely and look for any fleeting expressions that may contradict their verbal statements.

Observe the whole face: While microexpressions are primarily seen in the face, it's important to consider the entire context. Pay attention to other nonverbal cues such as body posture, hand movements, and vocal tone, as they can provide additional clues to a person's true emotions.

Look for inconsistencies: When someone is being deceptive, there may be inconsistencies between their verbal and nonverbal cues. For example, they may say they are happy while displaying a microexpression of sadness. Look for these incongruences as they can indicate deception.

Practice empathy: Empathy can help you better understand and interpret microexpressions. Try to envision what the other person might be going through by placing yourself in their position. This can help you identify and interpret their microexpressions more accurately.

Use video resources: Watching videos or movies that depict real-life situations can be a helpful way to practice recognizing microexpressions. Pause the video at different points and try to identify the microexpressions displayed by the characters.

Seek professional training: If you are interested in becoming more proficient in reading microexpressions and detecting deception, consider seeking professional training. There are courses and workshops available that can provide you with the necessary skills and knowledge.

Ethical Considerations

While the ability to read microexpressions and detect deception can be valuable in certain contexts, it is important to approach this skill with ethical considerations in mind. It is crucial to use this knowledge responsibly and not to make unfounded accusations or assumptions based solely on microexpressions.

Microexpressions are just one piece of the puzzle when it comes to understanding a person's true emotions and intentions. It is essential to consider other factors such as verbal statements, body language, and the overall context before drawing any conclusions.

By developing your skills in recognizing microexpressions and understanding deceptive behaviors, you can enhance your ability to interpret body language accurately. This can be particularly useful in situations where detecting deception is important, such as in negotiations, interviews, or personal relationships. Always remember to approach this skill with empathy, integrity, and respect for others.

Body Language Clues to Detecting Lies

Detecting deception can be a challenging task, but by understanding the body language clues associated with lying, you can significantly improve your ability to read people and uncover the truth. While it is important to remember that body language alone cannot definitively prove someone is lying, it can provide valuable insights into their thoughts and emotions.

Facial Expressions

Facial expressions are one of the most significant indicators of deception. When someone is lying, they may display microexpressions, which are brief and involuntary facial expressions that reveal their true emotions. These microexpressions can occur within a fraction of a second and are often difficult to detect. With practice and observation, you can learn to spot them.

Some common facial expressions associated with lying include:

Microexpressions of fear: When someone is lying, they may briefly display a microexpression of fear, indicating their anxiety about being caught in a lie.

Lack of facial expression: Liars may try to control their facial expressions to avoid giving away their true emotions. As a result, their faces may appear relatively blank or lacking in expression.

Incongruent expressions: Pay attention to inconsistencies between a person's facial expressions and their verbal statements. If their words and facial expressions do not align, it could be a sign of deception.

Eye Movements and Gaze

The eyes can provide valuable clues about a person's truthfulness. While it is a common belief that liars avoid eye contact, this is not always the case. Some individuals may increase their eye contact to appear more trustworthy. There are other eye movements and gaze patterns that can indicate deception:

Rapid eye blinking: Excessive blinking or rapid eye movements can be a sign of nervousness or anxiety, which may indicate that someone is lying.

Avoidance of eye contact: While not always a reliable indicator, avoiding eye contact can be a sign of discomfort or dishonesty. Liars may try to avoid direct eye contact to reduce the chances of being detected.

Prolonged eye contact: On the other hand, some individuals may try to overcompensate by maintaining prolonged eye contact to appear more sincere. This intense gaze can be a deliberate attempt to deceive.

Body Movements and Gestures

A person's body movements and gestures can also provide valuable insights into their truthfulness. Observe the following body language cues:

Fidgeting and restlessness: Liars may exhibit increased fidgeting, such as tapping their fingers, shaking their legs, or playing with objects. Restlessness can be a sign of nervousness and discomfort associated with lying.

Defensive postures: When someone is lying, they may adopt defensive postures, such as crossing their arms, hunching their shoulders, or creating physical barriers between themselves and others. These defensive gestures can indicate a subconscious attempt to protect themselves from being exposed.

Excessive hand movements: Liars may use excessive hand movements to distract or divert attention away from their deception. These gestures can be exaggerated and unrelated to the conversation at hand.

Verbal and Nonverbal Incongruence

When trying to detect lies, it is essential to pay attention to the congruence between a person's verbal and nonverbal cues. Incongruence occurs when there is a mismatch between what someone is saying and how they are expressing themselves nonverbally. Some examples of incongruence include:

Contradictory gestures: If someone is verbally denying something while nodding their head in agreement, it could be a sign of deception. Incongruent gestures can reveal their true feelings or thoughts.

Inconsistent tone of voice: Pay attention to changes in a person's tone of voice. Sudden shifts in pitch, volume, or speed can indicate discomfort or an attempt to deceive.

Inappropriate laughter: Sometimes, individuals may laugh or smile inappropriately when lying. This laughter can be a nervous response or an attempt to downplay the seriousness of the situation.

It is important to note that these body language cues should be interpreted in clusters rather than in isolation. A single gesture or expression may not necessarily indicate deception, but when multiple cues align, it can provide a more accurate assessment.

Body language is not a precise science when it comes to detecting lies. People's behaviors can vary, and cultural differences can influence how individuals express themselves. Therefore, it is crucial to consider the context, baseline behavior, and individual differences when interpreting body language cues.

By developing your observation skills and understanding the body language clues associated with deception, you can enhance your ability to read people and uncover the truth. However, it is essential to approach this skill with caution and use it responsibly, always considering the potential for misinterpretation.

Interpreting Incongruence in Verbal and Nonverbal Communication

In the previous sections, we have discussed the various aspects of body language and how it can be used to detect deception. It is important to note that sometimes there can be inconsistencies or incongruence between a person's verbal and nonverbal communication. These inconsistencies can provide valuable insights into a person's true thoughts and feelings.

Understanding Incongruence

Incongruence refers to the mismatch or misalignment between a person's verbal and nonverbal communication. It occurs when someone's words do not align with their body language, facial expressions, or other nonverbal cues. This inconsistency can be a result of various factors, such as discomfort, deception, or conflicting emotions.

When interpreting incongruence, it is essential to consider the context and the individual's baseline behavior. Everyone has their unique way of expressing themselves, and what may be incongruent for one person may be normal for another. Therefore, it is crucial to establish a baseline understanding of a person's typical behavior before making any judgments.

Signs of Incongruence

Several signs can indicate incongruence between verbal and nonverbal communication. These signs can help you identify when someone may not be expressing their true thoughts or feelings. Here are a few typical indicators to watch out for:

Inconsistent facial expressions: Pay attention to the person's facial expressions while they are speaking. If their words convey one emotion, but their facial expressions show a different emotion, it may indicate incongruence.

Contradictory gestures: Observe the person's gestures and body movements. If their gestures contradict their words or convey a different message, it can be a sign of incongruence.

Inappropriate laughter or smiles: Sometimes, people may use laughter or smiles as a way to mask their true emotions. If someone laughs or smiles in situations where it is not appropriate, it may indicate incongruence.

Inconsistent eye contact: Eye contact is an essential aspect of nonverbal communication. If someone avoids eye contact or their eye contact does not match their words, it can be a sign of incongruence.

Verbal and nonverbal cues that do not align: Pay attention to any inconsistencies between a person's words and their nonverbal cues. For example, if someone says they are happy but their body language suggests otherwise, it may indicate incongruence.

Interpreting Incongruence

Interpreting incongruence requires careful observation and analysis of both verbal and nonverbal cues. Here are some steps to help you interpret incongruence effectively:

Pay attention to clusters of cues: Look for patterns or clusters of incongruent cues rather than relying on a single cue. Multiple incongruent cues can provide stronger evidence of incongruence.

Consider the context: Take into account the context in which the incongruence is occurring. Different situations can elicit different responses, and what may seem incongruent in one context may be normal in another.

Trust your intuition: While it is important to analyze and interpret cues objectively, it is also essential to trust your intuition. Sometimes, your gut feeling can provide valuable insights into incongruence.

Seek clarification: If you notice incongruence in someone's communication, it can be helpful to seek clarification. Ask open-ended questions to encourage the person to provide more information and potentially reveal their true thoughts or feelings.

Consider cultural differences: Keep in mind that cultural differences can influence the way people express themselves. What may appear incongruent in one culture may be perfectly normal in another. Be mindful of cultural nuances when interpreting incongruence.

The Importance of Incongruence in Communication

Understanding and interpreting incongruence in verbal and nonverbal communication can provide valuable insights into a person's true thoughts, feelings, and intentions. It allows you to go beyond the surface level and gain a deeper understanding of what someone is truly trying to convey.

By recognizing incongruence, you can become a more effective communicator and build stronger connections with others. It enables you to detect potential deception, understand hidden emotions, and respond appropriately in various social and professional situations.

Interpreting incongruence in verbal and nonverbal communication is an essential skill in mastering the art of body language. By paying attention to the signs of incongruence and analyzing the context, you can gain valuable insights into a person's true thoughts and feelings. This understanding can enhance your communication skills and help you navigate social interactions more effectively.

Chapter 6: Cultural Differences in Body Language

The Influence of Culture on Body Language

Culture plays a significant role in shaping our behavior and communication styles, including our body language. The way we express ourselves nonverbally can vary greatly across different cultures, and understanding these cultural differences is crucial for effective communication.

Cultural Norms and Body Language

Every culture has its own set of norms and values that dictate how individuals should behave and communicate. These cultural norms also extend to body language, influencing the way people use gestures, facial expressions, and other nonverbal cues to convey meaning.

For instance, maintaining direct eye contact is regarded as a respectful and attentive gesture in certain cultures. On the other hand, extended eye contact could be viewed as impolite or aggressive in other cultures. Similarly, the use of personal space can vary significantly across cultures. In some cultures, people may stand closer to each other during conversations, while in others, a larger personal space is preferred.

Understanding these cultural norms is essential to avoid misinterpretation and potential misunderstandings. When interacting with individuals from different cultural backgrounds, it is important to be aware of these differences and adapt our body language accordingly.

Cultural Body Language Gestures

Gestures are an integral part of nonverbal communication, and they can vary greatly across cultures. What may be considered a common gesture in one culture could have a completely different meaning in another. Here are a few examples of cultural body language gestures:

Hand gestures: The use of hand gestures can vary significantly across cultures. For instance, the "thumbs up" gesture is commonly used to indicate approval or agreement in Western cultures. However, in some Middle Eastern and

South American cultures, it can be seen as offensive or vulgar.

Nodding and shaking the head: The meaning of nodding and shaking the head can also differ across cultures. In Western cultures, nodding the head up and down typically signifies agreement or affirmation, while shaking the head from side to side indicates disagreement or negation. However, in some cultures, such as Bulgaria and Greece, nodding the head means "no," while shaking the head means "yes."

Bowing: Bowing is a common gesture in many Asian cultures, such as Japan and South Korea, to show respect and humility. The depth and duration of the bow can convey different levels of respect and formality.

Handshakes: The way people shake hands can also vary across cultures. In Western cultures, a firm handshake is generally seen as a sign of confidence and professionalism. However, in some Asian cultures, a softer handshake is preferred, as a firm grip may be considered aggressive or impolite.

These are just a few examples of how cultural differences can influence body language gestures. It is important to be mindful of these differences and avoid making assumptions based on our cultural norms.

Cross-Cultural Communication

When engaging in cross-cultural communication, it is crucial to be sensitive to cultural differences in body language. Here are some tips to navigate cross-cultural communication effectively:

Educate yourself: Take the time to learn about the cultural norms and body language gestures of the culture you will be interacting with. Understanding these differences will help you interpret and respond appropriately to nonverbal cues.

Observe and adapt: Pay attention to the body language of the individuals you are interacting with. Observe their gestures, facial expressions, and other nonverbal cues to gain insight into their communication style. Adapt your body language to align with their cultural norms, while remaining authentic.

Ask for clarification: If you are unsure about the meaning behind a particular gesture or nonverbal cue, don't hesitate to ask for clarification. People from different cultures are often willing to explain their customs and traditions, and this can help avoid misunderstandings.

Be patient and open-minded: Cross-cultural communication can sometimes be challenging, but it is important to approach it with patience and an open mind. Recognize that cultural differences exist and be respectful of them. Embrace the opportunity to learn from others and expand your cultural understanding.

Avoiding Misinterpretation in a Multicultural World

In today's interconnected world, we often find ourselves interacting with individuals from diverse cultural backgrounds. To avoid misinterpretation and foster effective communication, it is essential to be mindful of cultural differences in body language. Here are some additional strategies to consider:

Build relationships: Developing relationships with individuals from different cultures can help bridge the gap in understanding. By building trust and rapport, you create a safe space for open communication and can better navigate cultural differences.

Seek feedback: If you regularly interact with individuals from a particular culture, consider seeking feedback on your body language. Ask for their perspective on how you come across and if there are any cultural nuances you should be aware of.

Embrace diversity: Embrace the diversity of body language and communication styles. Recognize that there is no one "correct" way to express oneself nonverbally. By embracing diversity, you create an inclusive environment that values and respects different cultural perspectives.

Practice empathy: Put yourself in the shoes of others and try to understand their cultural background and experiences. Cultivating empathy allows you to approach cross-cultural communication with sensitivity and understanding.

By being aware of the influence of culture on body language and actively working to bridge cultural gaps, we can enhance our communication skills and build stronger connections with people from all walks of life.

Common Cultural Body Language Gestures

Body language is a powerful form of nonverbal communication that varies across different cultures. Understanding and interpreting these cultural body language gestures can help you navigate cross-cultural interactions and avoid misinterpretation.

Hand Gestures

Hand gestures are a universal form of communication, but their meanings can vary across cultures. Here are some examples of common hand gestures and their cultural interpretations:

Thumbs Up: In many Western cultures, a thumbs-up gesture is a sign of approval or agreement. However, in some Middle Eastern and West African countries, it can be seen as offensive or vulgar.

Okay, Sign: In Western cultures, forming a circle with your thumb and index finger to create the "okay" sign signifies that everything is fine or acceptable. However, in countries like Brazil, France, and Turkey, this gesture can be interpreted as an insult or vulgar gesture.

V Sign: In many Western countries, making a V sign with your index and middle fingers is a symbol of victory or peace. However, in some Asian countries like Japan and South Korea, it can be seen as an offensive gesture.

Handshake: The handshake is a common greeting gesture in many Western cultures. However, the firmness of the handshake can vary across cultures. In some cultures, a weak handshake may be seen as a sign of disrespect, while in others, an overly strong handshake may be considered aggressive.

Facial Expressions

Facial expressions play a crucial role in conveying emotions and intentions. Different cultures may interpret facial expressions differently. Here are some examples of cultural differences in facial expressions:

Smiling: While a smile is generally seen as a sign of happiness or friendliness, the frequency and meaning of smiling can vary across cultures. In some cultures, a smile may be used to mask negative emotions or as a sign of politeness, while in others, it may be seen as insincere or inappropriate.

Eye Contact: Eye contact is an important aspect of communication, but its significance varies across cultures. Keeping eye contact is commonly regarded as an indication of attentiveness and honesty in Western cultures. In some Asian cultures, prolonged eye contact may be considered disrespectful or confrontational.

Nodding: Nodding is commonly used to indicate agreement or understanding. However, the frequency and meaning of nodding can differ across cultures. In some cultures, nodding may be used to show respect or politeness, while in others, it may simply indicate attentiveness without necessarily implying agreement.

Posture and Body Movements

Posture and body movements can convey a wealth of information about a person's emotions, intentions, and social status. Here are some examples of cultural differences in posture and body movements:

Sitting Position: The way people sit can vary across cultures. In some cultures, sitting cross-legged or with legs crossed at the ankles is considered polite and respectful, while in others, it may be seen as casual or disrespectful.

Gesturing with Hands: The use of hand gestures while speaking can vary across cultures. In some cultures, using hand gestures to emphasize a point is common and encouraged, while in others, it may be seen as excessive or distracting.

Personal Space: The concept of personal space, or the distance individuals prefer to keep between themselves and others, can vary across cultures. In some cultures, people may stand or sit closer to each other during conversations, while in others, a larger personal space is preferred.

Understanding these cultural differences in body language gestures can help you avoid misunderstandings and communicate effectively in cross-cultural situations. It is important to remember that these are generalizations, and individual preferences and interpretations may vary within a culture. When in doubt, it is always best to observe and adapt to the body language cues of the people you are interacting with.

By being aware of and respecting cultural differences in body language, you can enhance your cross-cultural communication skills and build stronger connections with people from different backgrounds.

Navigating Cross-Cultural Communication

Cross-cultural communication is an essential skill in today's globalized world. As we interact with people from different cultures, it is crucial to understand and navigate the nuances of body language to ensure effective communication. Body language varies across cultures, and what may be considered acceptable or appropriate in one culture may be perceived differently in another.

Understanding Cultural Differences

To navigate cross-cultural communication successfully, it is essential to have a basic understanding of cultural differences. Different cultures have unique norms, values, and beliefs that influence their body language. For example, in some cultures, maintaining direct eye contact is a sign of respect and attentiveness, while in others, it may be seen as confrontational or disrespectful.

It is crucial to research and familiarize yourself with the cultural norms of the specific culture you are interacting with. This will help you avoid misunderstandings and misinterpretations of body language signals. Understanding the cultural context will enable you to adapt your body language and interpret the signals of others accurately.

Respect and Sensitivity

Respect and sensitivity are key when navigating cross-cultural communication. Approaching conversations with an open mind and a readiness to pick up new skills and adjust to changing circumstances is crucial. Avoid making assumptions or generalizations about a culture based on stereotypes. Instead, approach each interaction with curiosity and a genuine desire to understand and connect with others.

Be aware of your body language and how it may be perceived by individuals from different cultures. Make an effort to be respectful and sensitive to cultural norms, even if they differ from your own. This may involve adjusting your posture, gestures, or level of eye contact to align with the cultural expectations of the person or group you are communicating with.

Nonverbal Communication Cues

Nonverbal communication cues play a significant role in cross-cultural communication. While some body language signals may be universal, others can vary greatly across cultures. It is important to pay attention to these cues and interpret them within the cultural context.

For example, the meaning of a smile can differ across cultures. In some cultures, a smile may indicate happiness or friendliness, while in others, it may be used to mask discomfort or hide negative emotions. Similarly, the use of hand gestures can vary widely. A gesture that is innocuous in one culture may be offensive or inappropriate in another.

To navigate cross-cultural communication effectively, observe and learn from the nonverbal cues of individuals from different cultures. Pay attention to their facial expressions, gestures, and body posture. This will help you develop a better understanding of their communication style and enable you to adjust your body language accordingly.

Active Listening and Clarification

Active listening and clarification are essential skills when navigating cross-cultural communication. It is important to listen attentively to both verbal and nonverbal cues to gain a comprehensive understanding of the message being conveyed.

When interacting with individuals from different cultures, make an effort to clarify and confirm your understanding. This can be done by paraphrasing or summarizing what you have heard and observed. This not only demonstrates your engagement but also allows for any potential misunderstandings to be addressed and corrected.

Building Rapport and Trust

Building rapport and trust is crucial in cross-cultural communication. Nonverbal cues play a significant role in establishing rapport and creating a positive connection with others. By adapting your body language to align with the cultural norms of the individuals you are communicating with, you can build trust and foster a sense of mutual understanding.

To build rapport, mirror the body language of the person you are interacting with to a certain extent. This does not mean mimicking their every move but rather subtly matching their posture, gestures, and facial expressions. This mirroring technique can help create a sense of familiarity and connection.

It is important to be mindful of cultural differences and avoid overstepping boundaries. Adapt your body language respectfully and appropriately, taking into consideration the cultural context and the comfort level of the individuals you are communicating with.

Patience and Flexibility

Patience and flexibility are essential when navigating cross-cultural communication. It may take time to fully understand and adapt to the body language cues of different cultures. Navigating these differences requires patience, both with yourself and with others.

Flexibility is also key. Recognize that not all individuals from a particular culture will conform to the same body language norms. Just as there are variations within your own culture, there will be variations within other cultures as well. Be open to learning and adjusting your approach based on the specific individuals you are interacting with.

Seek Cultural Guidance

When navigating cross-cultural communication, it can be helpful to seek cultural guidance from individuals who are familiar with the culture you are interacting with. This can be done through research, reading books or articles, or even engaging in conversations with individuals from that culture.

By seeking cultural guidance, you can gain valuable insights into the body language norms and expectations of a particular culture. This knowledge will enable you to navigate cross-cultural communication more effectively and avoid potential misunderstandings.

Practice Empathy and Understanding

Practicing empathy and understanding is crucial when navigating cross-cultural communication. Recognize that individuals from different cultures may have different perspectives, values, and ways of expressing themselves. Approach each interaction with an open mind and a genuine desire to understand and connect with others.

By practicing empathy, you can develop a deeper understanding of the cultural nuances of body language and communicate more effectively across cultures. This will not only enhance your cross-cultural communication skills but also foster meaningful connections and relationships with individuals from diverse backgrounds.

Navigating cross-cultural communication through body language requires awareness, respect, and a willingness to learn. By understanding and adapting to cultural differences, actively listening and clarifying, building rapport and trust, practicing patience and flexibility, seeking cultural guidance, and practicing empathy and understanding, you can navigate cross-cultural communication successfully and foster meaningful connections with individuals from different cultures.

Avoiding Misinterpretation in a Multicultural World

In today's globalized world, it is becoming increasingly common to interact with people from different cultures and backgrounds. As a result, understanding and interpreting body language accurately can be challenging, as cultural norms and gestures can vary significantly. Misinterpreting body language can lead to misunderstandings, miscommunication, and even offense. Therefore, it is crucial to develop the skills to avoid misinterpretation in a multicultural world. In this section, we will explore some strategies to help you navigate cross-cultural communication effectively.

Cultivate Cultural Sensitivity

One of the most important steps in avoiding misinterpretation is to cultivate cultural sensitivity. Recognize that different cultures have their own unique set of nonverbal cues and gestures, and what may be considered acceptable in one culture may be offensive or inappropriate in another.

Take the time to educate yourself about the cultural norms and customs of the people you interact with. This can be done through reading, research, or even engaging in conversations with individuals from different cultures. By understanding and respecting cultural differences, you can minimize the chances of misinterpreting body language.

Be Mindful of Stereotypes

It is essential to be mindful of stereotypes when interpreting body language in a multicultural context. Stereotypes can lead to assumptions and biases, which can cloud your judgment and hinder effective communication. Avoid making generalizations about a person's body language based on their cultural background. Instead, focus on observing and understanding the individual's unique nonverbal cues within the context of their specific cultural norms. By approaching each interaction with an open mind, you can avoid misinterpretation and foster better understanding.

Seek Clarification

When in doubt, it is always better to seek clarification rather than make assumptions. If you are unsure about the meaning behind a particular gesture or body language signal, politely ask the person about its significance. Most people appreciate the opportunity to explain their cultural practices and will be happy to provide clarification. By engaging in open and respectful dialogue, you can bridge the gap of understanding and avoid misinterpretation.

Pay Attention to Context

Context plays a crucial role in interpreting body language accurately. Different situations and environments can influence the meaning behind certain gestures or expressions. For example, a smile may convey happiness in one context but could also be a sign of politeness or nervousness in another.

Pay attention to the overall context of the interaction, including the cultural setting, the relationship between the individuals involved, and the specific circumstances. By considering the broader context, you can gain a more accurate understanding of the intended message.

Develop Cross-Cultural Communication Skills

To avoid misinterpretation in a multicultural world, it is essential to develop cross-cultural communication skills. This involves being open-minded, adaptable, and willing to learn from others. Actively listen to the verbal and nonverbal cues of the person you are communicating with, and be aware of your body language to ensure it aligns with the cultural norms of the situation. Practice empathy and try to put yourself in the other person's shoes to gain a deeper understanding of their perspective. By continuously honing your cross-cultural communication skills, you can navigate diverse cultural contexts with confidence and sensitivity.

Be Respectful and Patient

Respect and patience are key when interacting with individuals from different cultures. Recognize that misunderstandings may occur, and it is essential to approach these situations with respect and understanding. If a misinterpretation does happen, remain calm and open to discussion.

Avoid blaming or criticizing the other person, as this can further escalate the situation. Instead, focus on finding common ground and working together to clarify any misunderstandings. By maintaining a respectful and patient attitude, you can foster positive and meaningful cross-cultural interactions.

Learn from Experience

The best way to avoid misinterpretation in a multicultural world is to learn from your experiences. Each interaction with individuals from different cultures provides an opportunity for growth and understanding. Reflect on your past experiences and identify any instances where misinterpretation occurred. Consider what you could have done differently and how you can apply those lessons moving forward. By continuously learning and adapting, you can become more proficient in reading and interpreting body language across cultures.

Avoiding misinterpretation in a multicultural world requires cultivating cultural sensitivity, being mindful of stereotypes, seeking clarification, paying attention to context, developing cross-cultural communication skills, being respectful and patient, and learning from experience. By following these strategies, you can enhance your ability to interpret body language accurately and navigate cross-cultural communication with confidence and respect.

Chapter 7: Improving Your Body Language

Awareness of Your Nonverbal Signals

To effectively read and interpret the body language of others, it is crucial to first develop an awareness of your nonverbal signals. Your body language can greatly influence how others perceive and respond to you, and by understanding and controlling your nonverbal cues, you can enhance your communication skills and improve your interactions with others.

The Power of Self-Awareness

Self-awareness is the foundation of understanding and improving your body language. It involves being conscious of your thoughts, feelings, and behaviors, as well as how they are expressed through your body. By developing self-awareness, you can gain insight into the messages you are sending through your nonverbal signals and make adjustments as needed.

Observing Your Body Language

One of the first steps in becoming aware of your nonverbal signals is to observe yourself in different situations. Pay attention to how you stand, sit, and move, as well as the facial expressions you make. Notice any patterns or habits that you may have developed over time.

Understanding the Impact of Body Language

Body language plays a significant role in communication, often conveying messages that are more powerful than words alone. It can influence how others perceive your confidence, credibility, and trustworthiness. By understanding the impact of body language, you can make conscious choices to project the desired image and effectively convey your message.

Identifying Nonverbal Cues

There are several key nonverbal cues that you should be aware of when observing your body language:

Facial Expressions

Your facial expressions can reveal a wealth of information about your emotions and attitudes. Pay attention to your smiles, frowns, raised eyebrows, and other facial movements. Are they congruent with your intended message?

Posture and Body Alignment

The way you hold yourself can communicate confidence or insecurity. Notice if you tend to slouch or stand tall, and how you position your body in different situations. A straight posture with an open chest can convey confidence and approachability.

Gestures

Hand gestures can add emphasis and clarity to your verbal message. Pay attention to the gestures you naturally use when speaking and consider whether they enhance or distract from your communication.

Eye Contact

Eye contact is a powerful nonverbal cue conveying interest, attentiveness, and sincerity. Notice how often you make eye contact with others and whether it is appropriate for the situation.

Voice Tone and Volume

Your voice tone and volume can greatly impact how your message is received. Pay attention to the pitch, pace, and volume of your voice, and consider whether it aligns with the intended message.

Managing Your Nonverbal Signals

Once you have identified your nonverbal cues, it is important to learn how to manage and control them effectively. Here are some strategies to help you improve your nonverbal communication:

Practice Self-Reflection

Regularly reflect on your nonverbal signals and consider how they may be perceived by others. Ask for feedback from trusted friends or colleagues to gain additional insights.

Observe Others

Pay attention to the body language of others, particularly those who are skilled communicators. Notice how they use their nonverbal cues to enhance their message and try to incorporate similar techniques into your communication style.

Seek Professional Help

If you struggle with certain aspects of your body language, such as maintaining eye contact or controlling nervous gestures, consider seeking professional help. A communication coach or therapist can provide guidance and techniques to help you improve.

Practice in Different Settings

Take opportunities to practice your nonverbal communication skills in various settings. This could include social gatherings, professional meetings, or even everyday interactions. The more you practice, the more natural and effective your nonverbal signals will become.

Developing an awareness of your nonverbal signals is a crucial step in mastering the art of body language. By understanding and controlling your body language, you can enhance your communication skills, build stronger relationships, and project the desired image to others. Body language is a powerful tool that can greatly influence how others perceive and respond to you, so it is worth investing time and effort into improving your nonverbal communication.

Using Body Language to Enhance Communication

Body language is a powerful tool that can greatly enhance communication. By understanding and utilizing the nonverbal signals we send, we can effectively convey our thoughts, feelings, and intentions to others.

Nonverbal Listening

One of the most important aspects of using body language to enhance communication is nonverbal listening. Nonverbal listening involves paying attention to the nonverbal cues that others are sending and using that information to better understand their thoughts and feelings.

When engaging in a conversation, it is crucial to observe the other person's body language. Pay attention to their facial expressions, gestures, and posture. These nonverbal cues can provide valuable insights into their emotions and attitudes. For example, a furrowed brow may indicate confusion or concern, while a relaxed posture and a smile may indicate comfort and agreement.

By actively listening to the nonverbal signals of others, we can gain a deeper understanding of their message and respond accordingly. This not only helps us to better connect with others but also allows us to adjust our body language to create a more positive and effective communication experience.

Mirroring and Matching

Mirroring and matching are a technique that involves subtly imitating the body language of the person you are communicating with. This technique can help establish rapport and create a sense of connection between individuals.

When mirroring and matching, it is important to be subtle and natural. Pay attention to the other person's body language and try to mimic their gestures, facial expressions, and even their posture. This can help create a sense of familiarity and trust, as it signals that you are on the same wavelength.

It is essential to use mirroring and matching with caution It is not appropriate to use it to trick or control other people.

Instead, it should be used as a tool to build rapport and enhance communication.

Open and Inviting Body Language

Using open and inviting body language is another effective way to enhance communication. Open body language involves keeping your arms uncrossed, maintaining eye contact, and facing the person you are communicating with directly. This signals that you are approachable, receptive, and interested in what the other person has to say.

It is important to be mindful of your facial expressions. Smiling and nodding can convey warmth and agreement, while a furrowed brow or a frown may indicate confusion or disagreement. By consciously controlling your facial expressions, you can create a positive and welcoming atmosphere for effective communication.

Using Gestures and Postures

Gestures and posture play a significant role in enhancing communication. They can help emphasize key points, convey emotions, and add clarity to your message.

When using gestures, it is important to be natural and purposeful. Steer clear of movements that overdo or distract from your message. Instead, use gestures that complement your words and help illustrate your point. For example, using your hands to demonstrate the size or shape of an object can make your message more vivid and memorable.

Posture also plays a crucial role in communication. Standing or sitting up straight conveys confidence and attentiveness, while slouching or hunching can give the impression of disinterest or lack of confidence. By maintaining good posture, you can project a positive image and enhance your communication effectiveness.

Paying Attention to Personal Space

Personal space is an important aspect of body language that can greatly impact communication. Different cultures and individuals have varying preferences when it comes to personal space, so it is important to be mindful of this when interacting with others.

Respecting personal space involves maintaining an appropriate distance from the person you are communicating with. A person may feel uneasy or intimidated if their personal space is invaded, and they may feel disconnected if they are too far away. By finding the right balance, you can create a comfortable and conducive environment for effective communication.

Using body language to enhance communication is a valuable skill that can greatly improve our interactions with others. By actively listening to nonverbal cues, mirroring and matching, using open and inviting body language, utilizing gestures and posture, and paying attention to personal space, we can create a positive and effective communication experience. Practice these techniques and observe the positive impact they have on your interactions with others.

Practicing Positive Body Language

Effective communication requires the use of positive body language. It not only helps you convey your message clearly but also creates a positive and welcoming environment for others. When you practice positive body language, you can build stronger connections, establish trust, and enhance your overall communication skills.

Maintaining Good Posture

One of the fundamental aspects of positive body language is maintaining good posture. Your posture conveys a lot about your assurance and confidence. When you stand or sit up straight, it not only makes you appear taller and more confident but also shows that you are attentive and engaged in the conversation. Slouching or hunching over can give the impression of disinterest or lack of confidence. By consciously practicing good posture, you can project a positive image and make a strong first impression.

Smiling and Eye Contact

A genuine smile can work wonders in creating a positive atmosphere. It not only makes you appear approachable and friendly but also helps to establish a connection with others. When you smile, it shows that you are open to communication and interested in the conversation. Maintaining eye contact while smiling can further enhance the impact of your positive body language. Eye contact conveys attentiveness and sincerity, making the other person feel valued and heard.

Open and Relaxed Body Language

To project positive body language, it is important to adopt an open and relaxed posture. Crossing your arms or legs can create a barrier and give the impression of defensiveness or disinterest. Instead, keep your arms relaxed by your sides or use open gestures to show that you are receptive to the conversation. Avoid fidgeting or excessive movements, as they can be distracting and convey nervousness. By consciously adopting open and relaxed body language, you can create a welcoming environment and encourage open communication.

Mirroring and Matching

Mirroring and matching body language is a powerful technique to establish rapport and build connections with others. When you mirror someone's body language, it shows that you are attentive and engaged in the conversation. Subtly matching their gestures, posture, and facial expressions can create a sense of familiarity and trust.

It is important to be subtle and not mimic the other person's body language exactly, as it can come across as insincere or mocking. By practicing mirroring and matching, you can enhance your ability to connect with others and create a positive impression.

Using Hand Gestures

Hand gestures can be a powerful tool to enhance your communication and convey your message effectively. When used appropriately, hand gestures can add emphasis, clarity, and enthusiasm to your speech It's crucial to utilize gestures sparingly and stay away from overly dramatic or distracting motions. Be mindful of cultural differences, as certain gestures may have different meanings in different cultures. By incorporating appropriate hand gestures into your communication, you can enhance your body language and make a positive impact on your audience.

Active Listening

Active listening is an essential component of positive body language. When you actively listen to someone, it shows that you are fully engaged and interested in what they have to say. To practice active listening, maintain eye contact, nod your head to show understanding, and provide verbal and nonverbal cues to indicate that you are actively processing the information.

Avoid interrupting or multitasking, as it can convey disinterest or lack of respect. By practicing active listening, you can strengthen your communication skills and build stronger connections with others.

Being Mindful of Your Tone of Voice

Your tone of voice plays a significant role in conveying your message and emotions. To project positive body language, it is important to be mindful of your tone and speak in a clear, confident, and friendly manner. Avoid speaking too softly or too loudly, as it can create a negative impression.

Be aware of your pace and rhythm of speech, as speaking too fast or too slow can affect the clarity and impact of your message. By practicing mindful and positive vocal communication, you can enhance your overall body language and effectively convey your message.

Practicing Empathy and Respect

Practicing empathy and respect is crucial in projecting positive body language. When you genuinely listen to others, show understanding, and validate their feelings, it creates a positive and supportive environment. Avoid judgmental or dismissive body language, such as rolling your eyes or crossing your arms, as it can undermine the trust and connection with others. By practicing empathy and respect, you can foster positive relationships and create a harmonious atmosphere.

Self-Awareness and Reflection

Self-awareness is key to improving your body language. Take the time to reflect on your nonverbal signals and identify any negative or ineffective habits. Pay attention to your body language in different situations and observe how others respond to it. Seek input from dependable people who may offer helpful critiques and recommendations for enhancements. By continuously practicing self-awareness and reflection, you can make conscious efforts to improve your body language and project a positive image.

Practicing positive body language is essential for effective communication and building strong relationships. By maintaining good posture, smiling, using open and relaxed body language, mirroring and matching, using appropriate hand gestures, practicing active listening, being mindful of your tone of voice, practicing empathy and respect, and cultivating self-awareness, you can enhance your body language skills and make a positive impact on others.

Positive body language not only benefits your personal and professional relationships but also contributes to your overall success and well-being.

Overcoming Body Language Barriers

Body language is a powerful form of nonverbal communication that can greatly impact our interactions with others. However, there are times when body language can create barriers in communication, leading to misunderstandings and misinterpretations.

Cultural Differences

One of the biggest challenges in interpreting body language is the influence of cultural differences. Different cultures have their own unique set of gestures, postures, and facial expressions that carry specific meanings. What may be considered a friendly gesture in one culture could be seen as offensive or disrespectful in another.

To overcome this barrier, it is important to educate yourself about the cultural norms and practices of the people you are interacting with. Take the time to learn about their body language cues and understand the meanings behind them. Avoid making assumptions based on your cultural background and be open to learning and adapting to different cultural contexts.

Individual Differences

Just as cultural differences can impact body language, individual differences also play a significant role. Each person has their unique way of expressing themselves through body language, influenced by factors such as personality, upbringing, and personal experiences. What may be a common gesture for one person may have a completely different meaning for another.

To overcome this barrier, it is important to approach each individual with an open mind and avoid making assumptions based on generalizations. Take the time to observe and understand the specific body language cues of the person you are interacting with. Pay attention to their facial expressions, gestures, and posture, and try to interpret them in the context of their individuality.

Emotional Barriers

Emotions can also create barriers in body language communication. When a person is experiencing strong emotions such as anger, sadness, or fear, their body language may become more guarded or defensive. This can make it difficult to accurately interpret their nonverbal cues and understand their true feelings.

To overcome this barrier, it is important to approach the person with empathy and understanding. Recognize that their emotions may be influencing their body language and be patient in your interactions. Give them the space and time they need to express themselves and try to create a safe and supportive environment for open communication.

Language Barriers

Language barriers can also impact the interpretation of body language. When two people do not share a common language, they may rely more heavily on nonverbal cues to communicate. Different cultures may have different interpretations of certain gestures or expressions, leading to misunderstandings.

To overcome this barrier, it is important to use clear and simple nonverbal cues that are universally understood. Focus on using gestures and facial expressions that are commonly recognized across cultures, such as a smile to indicate friendliness or a nod to show agreement. Using visual aids or props can help to enhance understanding and bridge the language gap.

Lack of Awareness

Sometimes, the biggest barrier in body language communication is our lack of awareness. We may be so focused on what we are saying or thinking that we fail to pay attention to the nonverbal cues of others. This may result in lost chances for communication and comprehension.

To overcome this barrier, it is important to cultivate mindfulness and present-moment awareness. Practice active listening and make a conscious effort to observe the body language of others. Pay attention to their facial expressions, gestures, and posture, and try to interpret their nonverbal cues in conjunction with their verbal communication. By being fully present in the moment, you can enhance your ability to read and respond to body language effectively.

Body language barriers can hinder effective communication and lead to misunderstandings. By understanding and overcoming these barriers, we can improve our ability to interpret and respond to nonverbal cues. Whether it is cultural differences, individual variations, emotional barriers, language barriers, or lack of awareness, being mindful and open-minded can help us navigate the complexities of body language and enhance our overall communication skills.

Chapter 8: Mastering Body Language in Everyday Life

Applying Body Language Skills in Relationships

Body language plays a crucial role in our everyday interactions, especially in relationships. Whether it's a romantic partnership, a friendship, or a family bond, understanding and effectively interpreting body language can significantly enhance communication and deepen connections.

Romantic Relationships

Romantic relationships are built on trust, understanding, and effective communication. Body language can provide valuable insights into the emotions and intentions of your partner, helping you navigate the complexities of a romantic bond.

Paying Attention to Nonverbal Cues

In a romantic relationship, it is essential to be attentive to your partner's nonverbal cues. Pay attention to their facial expressions, gestures, and posture, as they can reveal a wealth of information about their feelings and desires. For example, a genuine smile, maintaining eye contact, and open body posture can indicate interest, attraction, and comfort.

Establishing Emotional Connection

Body language can also be used to establish and strengthen emotional connections in a romantic relationship. Simple gestures like holding hands, hugging, or cuddling can convey love, affection, and support. Mirroring your partner's body language can create a sense of unity and understanding.

Resolving Conflict

During times of conflict, body language can either escalate or de-escalate the situation. It is crucial to be aware of your body language and ensure that it remains open, non-threatening, and receptive. Avoid crossing your arms, rolling your eyes, or displaying defensive postures, as these can intensify the conflict. Instead, maintain eye contact, use open gestures, and actively listen to your partner's concerns.

Friendships

Mutual trust, understanding, and shared experiences are the foundation of a friendship. Body language can play a significant role in strengthening these bonds and fostering deeper connections.

Active Listening

Active listening is a fundamental aspect of any friendship. When engaging in a conversation with a friend, use body language to demonstrate your attentiveness and interest. Maintain eye contact, nod your head to show understanding, and lean in slightly to convey engagement. These nonverbal cues communicate that you value their thoughts and opinions.

Building Trust

Trust is the foundation of any strong friendship. Body language can help build trust by displaying openness and honesty. Avoid crossing your arms or legs, as this can create a barrier between you and your friend. Instead, adopt an open posture, face them directly, and maintain eye contact. These nonverbal signals convey trustworthiness and sincerity.

Expressing Support and Empathy

In times of need, body language can be a powerful tool for expressing support and empathy. A comforting touch, a gentle pat on the back, or a warm hug can convey care and understanding. Mirroring your friend's body language can create a sense of empathy and solidarity.

Family Relationships

Family relationships are unique and complex, and body language can play a vital role in maintaining harmony and understanding within the family unit.

Nonverbal Affection

Physical touch is an essential aspect of family relationships. Hugs, kisses, and gentle touches can convey love, support, and reassurance. These nonverbal displays of affection can strengthen the bond between family members and create a sense of security.

Active Engagement

Active engagement is crucial in family relationships, especially during conversations and family gatherings. Use body language to demonstrate your interest and engagement. Maintain eye contact, nod your head, and lean in slightly to show that you are actively listening and participating in the conversation.

Respecting Boundaries

Respecting personal boundaries is essential in family relationships. Pay attention to your family member's body language and be mindful of their personal space. If they display signs of discomfort or withdrawal, give them the space they need and avoid invading their boundaries.

Applying body language skills in relationships can significantly enhance communication, deepen connections, and foster understanding. Whether it's a romantic relationship, a friendship, or a family bond, being aware of nonverbal cues and effectively interpreting them can lead to healthier and more fulfilling relationships. By paying attention to body language, establishing emotional connections, resolving conflicts, and expressing support, we can master the art of body language in our everyday interactions.

Using Body Language in Professional Settings

Success in work environments depends on having great communication. While verbal communication plays a significant role, nonverbal cues, such as body language, can also greatly impact how others perceive us and the messages we convey. Understanding and utilizing body language in professional settings can help you build rapport, establish credibility, and enhance your overall communication skills.

Establishing a Positive First Impression

First impressions are formed within seconds of meeting someone, and body language plays a key role in this process. When entering a professional setting, it is important to project confidence and professionalism through your body language. Here are some tips to help you establish a positive first impression:

Maintain good posture: Stand or sit up straight, with your shoulders back and your head held high. Good posture conveys confidence and professionalism.

Make eye contact: Establishing and maintaining eye contact shows that you are engaged and interested in the conversation. Be mindful not to stare excessively, as it can make others uncomfortable.

Offer a firm handshake: When greeting someone, a firm handshake can convey confidence and trustworthiness. Ensure that your handshake is neither too weak nor too strong.

Smile: A genuine smile can help create a positive and welcoming atmosphere. It also signals that you are approachable and friendly.

Active Listening and Nonverbal Cues

Active listening is an essential skill in professional settings. It involves not only hearing the words being spoken but also paying attention to the speaker's nonverbal cues. By observing and interpreting these cues, you can gain a deeper understanding of the speaker's message and respond appropriately. The following are some nonverbal clues to be aware of:

Facial expressions: The face is an effective medium for expressing feelings. Pay attention to the speaker's facial expressions, as they can provide valuable insights into their thoughts and feelings.

Gestures: Hand movements and gestures can enhance or reinforce verbal communication. They can also indicate enthusiasm, emphasis, or agreement. Be cautious of excessive or distracting gestures that may detract from your message.

Body posture: The way a person holds their body can reveal their level of engagement and interest. Leaning forward slightly and facing the speaker demonstrates attentiveness, while crossing your arms or leaning back may indicate disinterest or defensiveness.

Nodding and other affirmations: Nodding your head or using other affirmations, such as "mm-hmm" or "I see," shows that you are actively listening and understanding the speaker's message. These cues encourage the speaker to continue and feel validated.

Adapting to Different Communication Styles

In professional settings, you may encounter individuals with different communication styles. Adapting your body language to match their style can help establish rapport and facilitate effective communication. Here are some tips for adapting to different communication styles:

Observe and mirror: Pay attention to the other person's body language and subtly mirror their gestures and posture. This can create a sense of familiarity and rapport, making the other person more comfortable.

Be mindful of personal space: Different cultures and individuals have varying expectations of personal space. Respect others' boundaries by maintaining an appropriate distance during conversations.

Listen actively: Show genuine interest in what the other person is saying by maintaining eye contact, nodding, and using appropriate facial expressions. This demonstrates that you value their input and encourage open communication.

Adjust your tone and pace: Match your tone and pace of speech to the other person's. If they speak softly and slowly, adopting a similar style can help establish a connection. Similarly, if they speak quickly and energetically, adjusting their pace can enhance communication.

Managing Body Language in Meetings and Presentations

Meetings and presentations are common in professional settings, and your body language can greatly impact how your message is received. Here are some tips for managing your body language in these situations:

Maintain an open posture: Avoid crossing your arms or legs, as it can create a barrier between you and others. Instead, keep your body open and facing towards the speaker or audience.

Use appropriate hand gestures: Hand gestures can enhance your message and make it more engaging. Watch out for too-dramatic or distracting motions that could take attention away from your message.

Control nervous habits: It is natural to feel nervous in high-pressure situations, but try to avoid nervous habits such as fidgeting, tapping your foot, or playing with objects. These behaviors can be distracting and convey a lack of confidence.

Use confident body language: Stand tall, make eye contact, and speak with a clear and confident voice. These cues convey authority and credibility, helping you establish a strong presence in meetings and presentations.

By understanding and utilizing body language in professional settings, you can enhance your communication skills, build stronger relationships, and achieve greater success in your career. Be mindful of both your body language and the nonverbal cues of others, as they can greatly impact the effectiveness of your communication.

Reading Body Language in Social Situations

In social situations, being able to read and interpret body language can greatly enhance your understanding of others and improve your communication skills. Whether you are at a party, a networking event, or simply having a conversation with friends, being able to accurately read body language can provide valuable insights into people's thoughts, feelings, and intentions.

Observing Facial Expressions

Facial expressions are one of the most important aspects of body language in social situations. They can reveal a person's emotions, attitudes, and reactions. By paying attention to facial expressions, you can gain valuable insights into how someone is feeling and how they are responding to the conversation or situation.

When observing facial expressions, it is important to consider both the individual features and the overall expression. For example, a raised eyebrow may indicate surprise or skepticism, while a smile can indicate happiness or friendliness. It is essential to remember that facial expressions can vary across cultures, so it is important to consider cultural differences when interpreting them.

Interpreting Gestures and Postures

Gestures and posture can also provide valuable information about a person's thoughts and feelings in social situations. Pay attention to how someone is using their hands, arms, and body to express themselves. For example, crossed arms may indicate defensiveness or discomfort, while open and relaxed body language can indicate openness and engagement.

It is important to consider the context when interpreting gestures and posture. For example, a person who is leaning forward and making eye contact may be showing interest and attentiveness, while someone who is slouching and avoiding eye contact may be disengaged or uninterested.

Noticing Eye Contact and Gaze

Eye contact and gaze can reveal a lot about a person's level of engagement and interest in a social situation. Maintaining eye contact can indicate attentiveness and sincerity, while avoiding eye contact may suggest discomfort or dishonesty. It is important to note that cultural norms and individual preferences can influence eye contact, so it is essential to consider these factors when interpreting eye contact and gaze.

Pay attention to where someone is looking. For example, if someone is consistently looking around the room, they may be bored or disinterested in the conversation. On the other hand, if someone is focused on you and maintaining eye contact, they are likely engaged and interested in what you have to say.

Sensing Touch and Personal Space

Touch and personal space can also provide important cues in social situations. Different cultures and individuals have varying comfort levels with touch and personal space, so it is important to be mindful of these differences. In general, invading someone's personal space or touching them without their consent can be seen as intrusive or inappropriate.

Pay attention to how someone reacts to touch or personal space violations. If someone pulls away or becomes visibly uncomfortable, it is a clear sign that their boundaries have been crossed. Conversely, if someone initiates touch or maintains proximity, it can indicate a level of comfort and trust.

Considering Context and Clusters of Signals

When reading body language in social situations, it is crucial to consider the context and look for clusters of signals. A single gesture or expression may not provide a complete picture, but when multiple signals align, they can provide a more accurate understanding of someone's thoughts and feelings.

For example, if someone is fidgeting, avoiding eye contact, and crossing their arms, it may indicate discomfort or defensiveness. On the other hand, if someone is smiling, making eye contact, and leaning forward, it may indicate interest and engagement.

Practicing Empathy and Active Listening

To effectively read body language in social situations, it is important to practice empathy and active listening. Empathy allows you to put yourself in someone else's shoes and understand their perspective, which can help you interpret their body language more accurately. Active listening involves giving your full attention to the person speaking, both verbally and nonverbally, and responding appropriately.

By practicing empathy and active listening, you can create a safe and supportive environment that encourages open communication and allows you to better understand and connect with others.

Being Mindful of Cultural Differences

When reading body language in social situations, it is crucial to be mindful of cultural differences. Different cultures have varying norms and expectations regarding body language, and what may be considered appropriate or meaningful in one culture may be completely different in another.

To avoid misinterpretation and cultural misunderstandings, take the time to educate yourself about the cultural norms of the people you interact with. Be open-minded and respectful of these differences, and always consider cultural context when interpreting body language.

Practicing and Refining Your Skills

Reading body language in social situations is a skill that can be developed and refined with practice. Take every opportunity to observe and analyze the body language of others in different social settings. Pay attention to your body language as well, as self-awareness is key to understanding how your nonverbal signals may be perceived by others.

Consider seeking feedback from trusted friends or mentors who can provide insights into your body language and help you identify areas for improvement. There are numerous resources available, such as books, online courses, and workshops, that can provide further guidance and techniques for mastering the art of reading body language.

By continuously practicing and refining your skills, you can become more proficient in reading body language in social situations, leading to improved communication, stronger relationships, and a deeper understanding of those around you.

Becoming a Body Language Expert

Becoming a body language expert takes time, practice, and a keen eye for detail. It requires a deep understanding of human behavior and the ability to interpret nonverbal cues accurately.

Study the Basics

To become proficient in reading body language, it is essential to start with a solid foundation. Begin by studying the basics of body language, such as facial expressions, gestures, posture, eye contact, and touch. Familiarize yourself with the common body language signals and their meanings. Understanding the fundamentals will provide you with a framework to build upon as you delve deeper into the subject.

Observe and Analyze

One of the most effective ways to become a body language expert is to observe and analyze people's behavior in various situations. Pay close attention to the nonverbal cues they display during conversations, meetings, or social interactions.

Observe their facial expressions, hand movements, body posture, and eye contact. Take note of any patterns or inconsistencies in their body language. The more you practice observing and analyzing, the better you will become at deciphering the hidden messages behind people's nonverbal cues.

Develop Empathy

Empathy plays a crucial role in understanding body language. By putting yourself in someone else's shoes, you can gain a deeper understanding of their emotions and motivations. Developing empathy allows you to connect with others on a more profound level and interpret their body language more accurately. Practice active listening and try to understand the underlying emotions behind the nonverbal cues you observe. This empathetic approach will enhance your ability to read body language effectively.

Learn from Experts

To accelerate your learning process, seek out experts in the field of body language. Read books, attend workshops, or watch videos by renowned body language experts. Learn from their experiences and insights. They can provide valuable tips and techniques that can help you refine your skills.

Consider joining online forums or communities where you can interact with like-minded individuals who share your interest in body language. Engaging in discussions and exchanging knowledge with others can further enhance your expertise.

Practice with Different People

To become a proficient body language expert, it is essential to practice reading body language with a diverse range of individuals. Each person has unique nonverbal cues, influenced by their personality, cultural background, and upbringing. By interacting with people from different walks of life, you will expose yourself to a wide array of body language signals. This exposure will help you develop a more comprehensive understanding of nonverbal communication and improve your ability to interpret body language accurately.

Video Analysis

Recording and analyzing videos of yourself or others can be a valuable tool in becoming a body language expert. By reviewing the footage, you can observe and analyze nonverbal cues in a more detailed manner. Pay attention to microexpressions, subtle gestures, and changes in body posture.

Video analysis allows you to pause, rewind, and replay specific moments, enabling you to capture nuances that may have gone unnoticed in real-time interactions. This practice will sharpen your observation skills and enhance your ability to read body language effectively.

Seek Feedback

To gauge your progress and identify areas for improvement, seek feedback from trusted individuals. Ask friends, family members, or mentors to provide honest feedback on your body language reading skills. They can offer valuable insights and point out any blind spots or biases you may have. Constructive feedback will help you refine your techniques and become more accurate in interpreting nonverbal cues.

Continuous Learning

Becoming a body language expert is an ongoing process. Stay curious and committed to continuous learning. Keep up with the latest research, studies, and developments in the field of body language. Attend seminars, workshops, or conferences to expand your knowledge and network with other experts. By staying updated and continuously honing your skills, you can maintain your expertise and adapt to discoveries in the field.

Apply Your Knowledge

The true test of becoming a body language expert is the ability to apply your knowledge in real-life situations. Practice reading body language in various contexts, such as social interactions, professional settings, or public speaking engagements.

Use your expertise to enhance your communication skills, build stronger relationships, and make more accurate judgments about others' intentions and emotions. The more you apply your knowledge, the more confident and proficient you will become as a body language expert.

Becoming a body language expert is a journey that requires dedication, practice, and a genuine interest in understanding human behavior. By following these strategies and techniques, you can develop the skills necessary to read body language accurately and become a true expert in the field. Body language is a powerful form of communication, and mastering it can significantly enhance your personal and professional relationships.

Conclusion

As we conclude our journey through HOW TO READ BODY LANGUAGE: Unlock the Secrets of Effective Communication and Deepen Your Connections by Analyzing Nonverbal Signals, I invite you to reflect on the transformative insights gained on this odyssey into the realm of nonverbal communication.

In these pages, we've unraveled the intricacies of facial expressions, gestures, and postures—the silent symphony that accompanies every spoken word. You are now equipped with the keys to deciphering this profound language, opening doors to a new level of understanding in your personal and professional relationships.

The art of reading body language is not just about acquiring a skill; it's about fostering genuine connections. As you navigate the complexities of human interaction, remember that every raised eyebrow, every subtle shift in gaze, tells a story. Your newfound ability to interpret these stories will not only enhance your communication but deepen your connections in ways you never thought possible.

In the grand finale of our exploration, I encourage you to continue practicing the principles shared within these chapters. Observe, listen, and feel the unspoken currents that weave through every encounter. Embrace the power you now hold to create connections that transcend words, forging bonds that resonate on a profound level.

Thank you for embarking on this journey with me. May the wisdom gained within these pages serve as a compass, guiding you towards a world where communication is an art form, and connections are the masterpiece. The language of the heart speaks without words—embrace it, live it, and watch your connections flourish.